ORDINARY AFFECTS

ORDINARY AFFECTS ● KATHLEEN STEWART

DUKE UNIVERSITY PRESS DURHAM & LONDON 2007

© 2007 Duke University Press

All rights reserved

9780822341079

Designed by C. H. Westmoreland

Typeset in Adobe Garamond with Orator display by
Tseng Information Systems, Inc.

Library of Congress Cataloging-in-Publication
Data appear on the last printed page of this book.

for ARIANA CLAIRE STEWART

CONTENTS

ACKNOWLEDGMENTS

I am grateful to the National Endowment for the Humanities for a fellowship year at the School of American Research in Santa Fe; to the University of California, Irvine, Humanities Institute for six months in Orange County; and to the University of Texas for a Dean's Fellowship and a Faculty Research Assignment.

Versions of various small parts of this book have been published elsewhere, as follows: *Annual Review of Anthropology* 28 (1999); *Intimacy*, ed. Lauren Berlant (Chicago: University of Chicago Press, 2000); *Cultural Studies and Political Theory*, ed. Jodi Dean (Ithaca: Cornell University Press, 2000); *Cross Cultural Poetics* 3, no. 3 (2000); *Modernism, Inc.: Essays on American Modernity*, ed. Jani Scanduri and Michael Thurston (New York: New York University Press, 2002); "Public Sentiments: Memory, Trauma, History, Action," ed. Ann Cvetkovich and Ann Pelegrini, special issue of *Scholar and Feminist Online* 2, no. 1 (2003); *Aesthetic Subjects: Pleasures, Ideologies, and Ethics*, ed. Pamela Matthews and David McWhirter (Minneapolis: University of Minnesota Press, 2003); *Transparency and Conspiracy: Ethnographies of Suspicion in the New World Order*, ed. Harry G. West and Todd Sanders (Durham, N.C.: Duke University Press, 2003); *Histories of the Future*, ed. Susan Harding and Daniel Rosenberg (Durham, N.C.: Duke University Press, 2005); *Handbook of Qualitative Research*, ed. Norman Denzin and Yvonna Lincoln (London: Sage, 2005); and "Uncharted Territories: An Experiment in Finding Missing Cultural Pieces," ed. Orvar Lofgren, special issue, *Ethnologia Europea: Journal of European Ethnology* 1, no. 2 (2005).

Many people have read or listened to parts or all of the various versions of this book. I am especially grateful to Begoña Aretxaga,

Lauren Berlant, James Clifford, Ann Cvetkovitch, Steven Feld, Donna Haraway, Susan Harding, Mary Hufford, Laura Long, Jason Pine, Gretchen Ritter, Betsy Taylor, Greg Urban, and Scott Webel. From the start, the life and stories of Daniel Webb have been an inspiration for my work in this volume. Some excellent stories also came from Andrew Causey, who is permanently missed in the neighborhood, and one came from Penny Van Horn who is still an excellent presence even though I never see her. My mother, Claire, and my brothers, Frank and Michael, each contributed a story. Other members of my family also built, and continue to build, the affective and narrative ground on which this book roosts. The Public Feelings group at the University of Texas has been the most intellectually and affectively stimulating and supporting academic scene I have ever been part of. I thank Ken Wissoker for knowing what this project was about long ago and being there for it, so patient and clear. Ronn Dula, John Dula, and Ariana Stewart have spun around the thing, day to day, with grace, squeals of laughter and rage, rolled eyes, whispers, headaches, distractions, interruptions, and smiling eyes (or knowing smirks). Thank you for that.

Ordinary Affects is an experiment, not a judgment. Committed not to the demystification and uncovered truths that support a well-known picture of the world, but rather to speculation, curiosity, and the concrete, it tries to provoke attention to the forces that come into view as habit or shock, resonance or impact. *Something* throws itself together in a moment as an event and a sensation; a something both animated and inhabitable.

This book is set in a United States caught in a present that began some time ago. But it suggests that the terms neoliberalism, advanced capitalism, and globalization that index this emergent present, and the five or seven or ten characteristics used to summarize and define it in shorthand, do not in themselves begin to describe the situation we find ourselves in. The notion of a totalized system, of which everything is always already somehow a part, is not helpful (to say the least) in the effort to approach a weighted and reeling present. This is not to say that the forces these systems try to name are not real and literally pressing. On the contrary, I am trying to bring them into view as a scene of immanent force, rather than leave them looking like dead effects imposed on an innocent world.

The ordinary is a shifting assemblage of practices and practical knowledges, a scene of both liveness and exhaustion, a dream of escape or of the simple life.[1] Ordinary affects are the varied, surg-

---

[1] See Lauren Berlant's essay "Cruel Optimism" (*Differences*, forthcoming) for a brilliant discussion of how objects and scenes of desire matter not just because of their content but because they hold promise

ing capacities to affect and to be affected that give everyday life the quality of a continual motion of relations, scenes, contingencies, and emergences.[2] They're things that happen. They happen in impulses, sensations, expectations, daydreams, encounters, and habits of relating, in strategies and their failures, in forms of persuasion, contagion, and compulsion, in modes of attention, attachment, and agency, and in publics and social worlds of all kinds that catch people up in something that feels like *some*thing.[3]

Ordinary affects are public feelings that begin and end in broad circulation, but they're also the stuff that seemingly intimate lives are made of. They give circuits and flows the forms of a life. They can be experienced as a pleasure and a shock, as an empty pause or a dragging undertow, as a sensibility that snaps into place or a profound disorientation. They can be funny, perturbing, or traumatic. Rooted not in fixed conditions of possibility but in the actual lines of potential that a *something* coming together calls to mind and sets in motion, they can be seen as both the pressure points of events or banalities suffered and the trajectories that forces might take if they were to go unchecked. Akin to Raymond Williams's structures of feeling, they are "social experiences in solution"; they

---

in the present moment of a thing encountered and because they become the means of keeping whole clusters of affects magnetized to them.

[2] See Gilles Deleuze and Félix Guattari, *Anti-Oedipus: Capitalism and Schizophrenia*, vol. 1, trans. Brian Massumi (Minneapolis: University of Minnesota Press, 1983), and *A Thousand Plateaus: Capitalism and Schizophrenia*, vol. 2, trans. Robert Hurley, Mark Seem, and Helen R. Lane (Minneapolis: University of Minnesota Press, 1987).

[3] See Lauren Berlant's introduction to *Intimacy* (Chicago: University of Chicago Press, 2000) and her essays "Nearly Utopian, Nearly Normal: Post-Fordist Affect in *Rosetta* and *La Promesse*" (*Public Culture*, forthcoming) and "Slow Death" (*Critical Inquiry*, forthcoming) for discussions of an individual's abstract yet contingent desire to feel like he or she is "in" something or can recognize *some*thing.

"do not have to await definition, classification, or rationalization before they exert palpable pressures."[4] Like what Roland Barthes calls the "third meaning," they are immanent, obtuse, and erratic, in contrast to the "obvious meaning" of semantic message and symbolic signification.[5] They work not through "meanings" per se, but rather in the way that they pick up density and texture as they move through bodies, dreams, dramas, and social worldings of all kinds. Their significance lies in the intensities they build and in what thoughts and feelings they make possible. The question they beg is not what they might mean in an order of representations, or whether they are good or bad in an overarching scheme of things, but where they might go and what potential modes of knowing, relating, and attending to things are already somehow present in them in a state of potentiality and resonance.

Ordinary affects, then, are an animate circuit that conducts force and maps connections, routes, and disjunctures.[6] They are a kind of contact zone where the overdeterminations of circulations, events, conditions, technologies, and flows of power literally take place. To attend to ordinary affects is to trace how the potency of forces lies in their immanence to things that are both flighty and hardwired, shifty and unsteady but palpable too. At once abstract and concrete, ordinary affects are more directly compelling than ideologies, as well as more fractious, multiplicitous, and unpredictable than symbolic meanings. They are not the kind of analytic object that can be laid out on a single, static plane of analysis, and

[4] See Raymond Williams, *Marxism and Literature* (New York: Oxford University Press, 1977), 133, 132.

[5] Roland Barthes, "The Third Meaning: Research Notes on Some Eisenstein Stills," in *The Responsibility of Forms: Critical Essays on Music, Art, and Representation*, trans. Richard Howard (Berkeley: University of California Press, 1985), 318.

[6] See Nigel Thrift, *Knowing Capitalism* (London: Sage, 2005), for a discussion of how capitalism forms an "animate surface" to life.

they don't lend themselves to a perfect, three-tiered parallelism between analytic subject, concept, and world. They are, instead, a problem or question emergent in disparate scenes and incommensurate forms and registers; a tangle of potential connections. Literally moving things—things that are in motion and that are defined by their capacity to affect and to be affected—they have to be mapped through different, coexisting forms of composition, habituation, and event. They can be "seen," obtusely, in circuits and failed relays, in jumpy moves and the layered textures of a scene. They surge or become submerged. They point to the jump of something coming together for a minute and to the spreading lines of resonance and connection that become possible and might snap into sense in some sharp or vague way.

Models of thinking that slide over the live surface of difference at work in the ordinary to bottom-line arguments about "bigger" structures and underlying causes obscure the ways in which a reeling present is composed out of heterogeneous and noncoherent singularities. They miss how someone's ordinary can endure or can sag defeated; how it can shift in the face of events like a shift in the kid's school schedule or the police at the door. How it can become a vague but compelling sense that something is happening, or harden into little mythic kernels. How it can be carefully maintained as a prized possession, or left to rot. How it can morph into a cold, dark edge, or give way to something unexpectedly hopeful.

This book tries to slow the quick jump to representational thinking and evaluative critique long enough to find ways of approaching the complex and uncertain objects that fascinate because they literally hit us or exert a pull on us. My effort here is not to finally "know" them—to collect them into a good enough story of what's going on—but to fashion some form of address that is adequate to their form; to find something to say about ordinary affects by performing some of the intensity and texture that makes them habitable and animate. This means building an idiosyncratic map of connections between a series of singularities.[7] It means pointing always outward to an ordinary world whose forms of living are now being composed and suffered, rather than seeking the closure or clarity of a book's interiority or riding a great rush of signs to a satisfying end. In this book I am trying to create a contact zone for analysis.

The writing here has been a continuous, often maddening, effort to approach the intensities of the ordinary through a close ethnographic attention to pressure points and forms of attention and attachment. *Ordinary Affects* is written as an assemblage of disparate scenes that pull the course of the book into a tangle of trajectories, connections, and disjunctures. Each scene begins anew the approach to the ordinary from an angle set off by the scene's affects. And each scene is a tangent that performs the sensation that something is happening—something that needs attending to. From the perspective of ordinary affects, thought is patchy and material. It does not find magical closure or even seek it, perhaps only because it's too busy just trying to imagine what's going on.

I write not as a trusted guide carefully laying out the links between theoretical categories and the real world, but as a point of impact, curiosity, and encounter. I call myself "she" to mark the difference between this writerly identity and the kind of subject that arises as a daydream of simple presence. "She" is not so much a subject position or an agent in hot pursuit of something definitive as a point of contact; instead, she gazes, imagines, senses, takes on, performs, and asserts not a flat and finished truth but some possibilities (and threats) that have come into view in the effort to become attuned to what a particular scene might offer.

From the perspective of ordinary affects, things like narrative

---

[7] See John Rajchman, *The Deleuze Connections* (Cambridge, Mass.: MIT Press, 2000), 4–13, for a discussion of the analysis that works to make connections.

and identity become tentative though forceful compositions of disparate and moving elements: the watching and waiting for an event to unfold, the details of scenes, the strange or predictable progression in which one thing leads to another, the still life that gives pause, the resonance that lingers, the lines along which signs rush and form relays, the layering of immanent experience, the dreams of rest or redemption or revenge. Forms of power and meaning become circuits lodged in singularities. They have to be followed through disparate scenes. They can gather themselves into what we think of as stories and selves. But they can also remain, or become again, dispersed, floating, recombining—regardless of what whole or what relay of rushing signs they might find themselves in for a while.

Walter Benjamin's 1999 *Arcades Project* is one model of this kind of thinking: his nomadic tracing of dream worlds still resonant in material things; his process of writing captions to found fragments and snapshots gathered into a loose assemblage; the way his thought presses close to its objects in order to be affected by them.

Roland Barthes's *S/Z* and *A Lover's Discourse* are models too: his attunement to the movements, pleasures, and poetics of language and things; his sense of the expansive, irreducible nature of forms of signification; his attention to the fragments that comprise things; his notion of the *punctum*—the wounding, personally touching detail that establishes a direct contact.

Leslie Stern's *The Smoking Book* assembles an array of brief ficto-critical stories united only by some mention of smoking, embedding theory in the situations encountered. The result is a mass of resonances linking precise moments and states of desire through a single, thin line of connection. It leaves the reader with an embodied sense of the world as a dense network of mostly unknown links.

Michael Taussig's *My Cocaine Museum* and *The Magic of the State* and Alphonso Lingis's *Dangerous Emotions* and *Foreign Bodies* also serve here as examples of ficto-critical efforts to perform the intensity of circuits, surges, and sensations.

D. J. Waldie's *Holy Land: A Suburban Memoir* is a surreally realist chronicle of Lakewood, California, which in the 1950s was built, overnight, as the "world's largest" subdivision. Like the subdivision grid, Waldie's memoir is constructed out of tiny bits of personal narrative, hometown tales, and moments in the history of real estate development, all held together with the mortar of a singular though widespread form of ordinariness.

David Searcy's *Ordinary Horror* brilliantly performs the attachment to fantasy that arises out of mundane sights and situations. Many other novels, such as Edward Jones's *The Known World*, Ian McEwan's *Atonement*, or Khaled Hosseini's *The Kite Runner*, produce scenes of a world saturated by jumpy attunements.

Finally, Lauren Berlant's mode of thinking and writing on the affects of the present moment serves here as a direct inspiration and source of insight. In her work, the academic concept becomes something new and promising. Embedded in the intense and complex affective attunement of her writing, her concepts of the noncoherent, the incommensurate, and the scenic, as well as of attachment, intimacy, exhaustion, and the unlivable but animating desires for rest or for the simple life have sent me back to rethink scenes over and over again.

It's been years now since we've been watching.

Something surges into view like a snapped live wire sparking on a cold suburban street. You can stare at it, transfixed by its erratic thrashing. Or you can shake it off fast and finish your morning walk as planned, eyeing the thing as you pass on your way to the dog park.

At the park, there is talk, and the dogs run around madly, as if recharged.

The flashing up is real.

It is delusional.

The dogs take to sleeping in nervous fits and starts. They throw one eye open, raising a single eyebrow in hard surprise. They cower under legs for no good reason and whimper at the sound of branches brushing up against the bathroom window in the still of the night. But with a simple, reassuring look and a murmur in the ear, a kiss on the head, or the glimpse of a tail running by, they're off again, stretching their legs in sheer pleasure.

RUNNING IN ORDINARY TIME

Everyday life is a life lived on the level of surging affects, impacts suffered or barely avoided. It takes everything we have. But it also spawns a series of little somethings dreamed up in the course of things.

It grows wary and excited.

There are all the details of getting the rent money together or of home remodeling, getting messed up and recovering (or not), looking for love (or not), trying to get into something, or trying to get out of something you've gotten yourself into, shopping, hoping, wishing, regretting, and all the tortures of exclusion and inclusion, self and other, right and wrong, here and there.

The ordinary registers intensities—regularly, intermittently, urgently, or as a slight shudder.

We wish for the simple life that winks at us from someone else's beautiful flowerbeds. We flip off other drivers, eye strange or delicious characters on the subway or the street. We scan the headlines, read the luscious novels and sobering memoirs two pages at a time before falling asleep at night. We lose hours at a time disappeared into some pleasure or obsession, or flipping hamburgers or filing charts all afternoon to the point of literal senselessness.

Attention is distracted, pulled away from itself. But the constant pulling also makes it wakeful, "at attention." Confused but attuned.

We're busy if we're lucky.

For some, the everyday is a process of going on until something happens, and then back to the going on.

For others, one wrong move is all it takes.

Worries swirl around the bodies in the dark.

People bottom out watching daytime television.

Schedules are thrown up like scaffolding to handle work schedules and soccer practice or a husband quietly drinking himself to death in the living room.

We dream of getting by, getting on track, getting away from it all, getting real, having an edge, beating the system, being ourselves, checking out.

But first we take the hit, or dodge it.

A LITTLE ACCIDENT, LIKE ANY OTHER

Modes of attending to scenes and events spawn socialities, identities, dream worlds, bodily states and public feelings of all kinds.

None of this is simply "good" or "bad" but always, first, both powerful and mixed.

She's in a café in a small West Texas town. A place where ranchers hang out talking seed prices and fertilizer and strangers passing through town are welcome entertainment. The sun is going down and she's halfway through her fresh-killed steak and her baked potato when a biker couple comes in limping. All eyes rotate to watch them as they move to a table and sit down. Their hair is tousled, their clothes rumpled and torn. They talk intently, locking their startled eyes. When she walks past their table on her way out, they raise their heads to ask if she's heading out on the west road and if she can look for bike parts. They say they hit a deer coming into town and dumped their bike. The deer, they say, fared much worse.

The room comes to a dead stop. All eyes and ears tune in to the sentience of the crash still resonating in the bikers' bodies. Then, slowly, taking their sweet time, people begin to offer questions from their tables, drawing out the details. First there is just the simple will to know what happened. But the talk, once set in motion, expands into a thicket of stories and social maneuverings. There is talk of other collisions and strange events at that place on the west road. Some people make eye contact across the room. There are sly smiles of recognition. Little seeds of speculation begin to sprout. The scene in the restaurant becomes an ordinary maze of inspirations and experiments.

It's as if the singularity of the event has shaken things up, lightening the load of personal preoccupations and social ruts. As if everyone was just waiting for something like this to happen. A "we" of sorts opens in the room, charging the social with lines of potential.

As she leaves, she imagines how, in the days to come, people will keep their eyes open for bike parts when they travel the west road and how there will be more talk. Conversations will gather around the event and spin off into talk about the overpopulation of deer or the new law legalizing riding without a helmet. There might be talk of what parts would break in a speeding encounter with a deer caught in a headlight, or of who is a good mechanic and who doesn't know what he's talking about. Or talk might turn to the image of hitting the open road, or surviving the desert injured, or to abstract principles like freedom, fate, and recklessness.

But one way or another, the little accident will compel a response. It will shift people's life trajectories in some small way, change them by literally changing their course for a minute or a day.

The chance event might add a layer of conflict or daydream to things. It might unearth old resentments, or set off a search for lessons learned. It might pull the senses into alignment with simple choices or polemics: good luck and bad, laws and liberties, wild rides and common sense. But for now, at least, and in some small way in the future, too, the talk will secretly draw its force from the event itself resonating in bodies, scenes, and forms of sociality.

And the habit of watching for something to happen will grow.

TUNED IN

The ordinary is a circuit that's always tuned in to some little something somewhere.

A mode of attending to the possible and the threatening, it amasses the resonance in things.

It flows through clichés of the self, agency, home, a life.

It pops up as a dream. Or it shows up in the middle of a derailing. Or in a simple pause.

It can take off in flights of fancy or go limp, tired, done for now.

It can pool up in little worlds of identity and desire.

It can draw danger.

Or it can dissipate, leaving you standing.

CIRCUIT TROUBLE

She's visiting a place in the mountains where there is abject poverty and stereotypes so strong they thicken the air like a stench. Strangers passing through drop their jaws and lock their car doors tight.

Right now, Bobby is worried about the Whitakers because there's been trouble with some rich kids from town.

The Whitakers are wild looking. Everyone points to them as the incarnation of mountain stereotype. She remembers the first time she met them, years before, on a home visit to their tiny shack with a doctor from the local poor people's clinic. Mrs. Whitaker had congestive heart failure. She sat with her swollen ankles propped up in a beat-up recliner while four or five mute teenage boys ran in and out of the house gesticulating some kind of story. Three or four younger children sat on a mattress on the floor, smiling, curious.

Then the mother died. After a few months, the father put on an old cowboy hat and a beautiful red and yellow satin shirt with sequins and drifted off. Mary Jo, the oldest, was able to take care of the others, cashing their disability checks and walking every day to the little store at the end of the holler to get weenies, Ding Dongs, coffee, and little cans of sweet evaporated milk.

For years now, neighbors have been bringing them food and clothing, carrying them to the hospital, and fighting to keep them from being taken by the state and split up. Someone gave them an old trailer, now decayed and collapsing on the spot. Broken-down cars have piled up and the Whitaker boys are now grown men. Some of them have built their own tiny shacks, no bigger than the smallest of tool sheds. Driving past their place on the narrow dirt road now, you see several men and women standing frozen in the yard, watching you pass. If you wave, they'll smile and wave back. If you don't, they'll just stand there woodenly and stare at you.

Two of the women go to the Tommy Creek Free Will Good Hope Baptist Church next door. They testify in a language the others can't understand, even though speaking in tongues is a regular thing. This language seems like a special connection with the divine.

The trouble started when a visiting preacher from town spotted the Whitakers on his way to the Tommy Creek church and then went back and told his congregation. A church committee brought food and clothes. Bobby says they must have realized what they had here, because they came back at Christmas with a camera and shot a video to show the congregation. A group of teenage boys in the church were seized by the images, so one dark night they surged toward the Whitakers's place. They threw rocks at the shacks to draw them out. A few weeks later they were back, and this time the Whitaker men came out showing guns. Bobby is afraid that the next time the rich kids will be back shooting.

An escalating exchange is sparked by a visceral encounter of images. In a video that blankly records an arresting image, young embodiments of a mainstream in the making come face to face with an otherness that compels a closer look. The order of representation gives way to a more violently affective contact.

Calling out the Whitakers, the kids from town surge toward a scene of their own confident force. The Whitakers learn their part in the face of threat—the headlights shining in their sleepy eyes and the crack of hostile shouts.

SHORT CIRCUIT

Her brother makes foreman at GE after twenty some years on the line. His first job is to lay off a lot of the other guys. Guys with twenty or thirty years in. It's horrible (he's a storyteller). One man has a heart attack in his office, so he calls the ambulance. He finds counseling for others who are having anxiety attacks and severe confusion. One man needs suicide intervention after his wife kicks him out of the house.

Her brother's stories are shell-shocked and they have no endings. They leave you hanging.

There's a strike over healthcare cuts and job security. He and the other foremen have to cross the picket line. It's horrible. He's been a union steward. He's given union speeches. Now things are getting ugly. Something powerful and painful flashes through him.

Soon after, there's a call for a one-day national strike. He and some of the other foremen go to management. They say they're not comfortable crossing the picket line. They're told they can take a personal day. Lucky for them it's only one day.

They're a weak link in the chain of command. They're strong, brave, and scared. They've hit a wall in what they can and can't do. They're a short circuit in a flow. They're lucky.

THE POLITICS OF THE ORDINARY

The politics of ordinary affect can be anything from the split second when police decide to shoot someone because he's black and standing in a dark doorway and has something in his hand, to a moment when someone falls in love with someone else who's just come into view. Obviously, the differences matter. The politics of any surge depends on where it might go. What happens. How it plays itself out and in whose hands.

Ideologies happen. Power snaps into place. Structures grow entrenched. Identities take place. Ways of knowing become habitual at the drop of a hat. But it's ordinary affects that give things the quality of a *some*thing to inhabit and animate. Politics starts in the animated inhabitation of things, not way downstream in the various dreamboats and horror shows that get moving. The first step in thinking about the force of things is the open question of what counts as an event, a movement, an impact, a reason to react. There's a politics to being/feeling connected (or not), to impacts that are shared (or not), to energies spent worrying or scheming (or not), to affective contagion, and to all the forms of attunement and attachment. There's a politics to ways of watching and waiting for something to happen and to forms of agency—to how the mirage of a straightforward exercise of will is a flag waved in one situation and a vicious, self-defeating deflation in another (as when someone of no means has a get-rich-quick daydream—a daydream to be free at last—that ends them up in jail). There's a politics to difference in itself—the difference of danger, the difference of habit and dull routine, the difference of everything that matters.

THE NEED TO REACT

The hard, resilient need to react has become a charged habit.

For her, it started early. Because she was a girl. Because her family, like all families, built its skin around dramas and luminous little tales with shiny scenes and vibrant characters. And because the storytellers kept track of what happened to everyone—the ends they came to. (Which, of course, were never good.)

The social and natural worlds could be seen through the outlines of impacts suffered.

They registered, literally, in a kind of hauntedness, a being weighed down, a palpable reaction.

For years now her early childhood has been coming back to her as shocks of beauty, or beautiful shocks.

She remembers her kindergarten class walking back from Woolworth's, carrying a box of furry yellow chicks. The look of red tulips standing upright in her mother's garden is married to the taste of found raspberries and tart rhubarb ripped out of the ground when no one was looking and eaten with a spoonful of dirt.

The scene of her mother in a beautiful black dress and red lipstick getting ready to go out cuts to the brilliant blood exploding from the face of the boy next door when he fell from a cliff and landed face down on the cement in front of her. Then the scene cuts to the rhythm of shocks, days later, as her father and the other men tear the cliff apart boulder by boulder. Each time one hits the ground it shakes the glasses in the pantry with an impact that seems transformative.

There is a spectral scene of her little brother hunched over something in the row of pine trees that hug the house. She passes him on the way to school; on the way back at lunchtime, there is the sight of the house in flames and the driveway full of fire trucks with flashing red lights. The phrase "playing with matches" seems to be written across the blue sky in huge, white, cloud letters.

Or there is the day that all of her grandparents come to visit and they are floating up the treacherous driveway in a big, wide car. Then the wheels are sliding off the icy edge and the big car lurches to the edge of the cliff and hangs suspended. The white heads in the back seat sit very still while she runs, yelling for help.

There are her fingers crushed in the milk door on the landing, her screams stifled in a panic to keep the secret that there are wild rabbits running around in the cellar.

Sunday drives are ice cream cones dripping down sticky fingers in the back seat and the wordless theft of the baby's cone, silent tears running down fat cheeks. There is the unspoken agreement among the older kids not to alert the front seat.

There's the dreamy performance at the vfw hall. Her sister is the "cancan" girl covered in clanking cans, and she's the "balloon girl" dancing in floating plastic spheres to the lyrics of "Itsy Bitsy Teenie Weenie Yellow Polka Dot Bikini" while everyone laughs.

Later, there are Saturday mornings spent fidgeting at her grandmother's table while her mother and her aunts tell graphic stories prompted by the seemingly simple work of remembering kinship ties and married names—stories of alcoholism, accidents, violence, and cancers.

There are the nights walking the streets with her mother, peering into picture windows to catch a dreamy glimpse of scenes at rest or a telltale detail out of place. A lamp by a reading chair or a shelf of knickknacks on the wall, a chair overturned.

So still, like a postcard.

STILL LIFE

A still is a state of calm, a lull in the action. But it is also a machine hidden in the woods that distills spirits into potency through a process of slow condensation.

In painting, a still life is a genre that captures the liveness of inanimate objects (fruit, flowers, bowls) by suspending their sensory beauty in an intimate scene charged with the textures of paint and desire.

Hitchcock was a master of the still in film production. A simple pause of the moving camera to focus on a door or a telephone could produce a powerful suspense.

Ordinary life, too, draws its charge from rhythms of flow and arrest. Still lifes punctuate its significance: the living room strewn with ribbons and wine glasses after a party, the kids or dogs asleep in the back seat of the car after a great (or not so great) day at the lake, the collection of sticks and rocks resting on the dashboard after a hike in the mountains, the old love letters stuffed in a box in the closet, the moments of humiliation or shock that suddenly lurch into view without warning, the odd moments of spacing out when a strange malaise comes over you, the fragments of experience that pull at ordinary awareness but rarely come into full frame.

A still life is a static state filled with vibratory motion, or resonance. A quivering in the stability of a category or a trajectory, it gives the ordinary the charge of an unfolding.

It is the intensity born of a momentary suspension of narrative, or a glitch in the projects we call things like the self, agency, home, a life. Or a simple stopping.

When a still life pops up out of the ordinary, it can come as a shock or as some kind of wake-up call. Or it can be a scene of sheer pleasure—an unnamed condensation of thought and feeling. Or an alibi for all of the violence, inequality and social insanity folded into the open disguise of ordinary things. Or it can be a flight from numbing routine and all the self-destructive strategies of carrying on.

It can turn the self into a dreaming scene, if only for a minute.

DAY-TRIPPING

There was a time when the two women would go on day trips, traipsing around small Texas towns in various states of preservation and faded beauty. There were town squares rimmed with ornate, stone-cut German buildings from the nineteenth century, now hosting gift shops or a local campaign headquarters. There were serendipitous scenes like the café that featured pies piled high with whipped cream and butter icing and where the waitress described every ingredient in supple, loving detail. Or the antique shop where a woman with big hair and a big accent described the ancient armoires and gilded birdcages that went for a song at last night's auction. People came from all around and left with their arms full.

There was the little police station where the two women went to find a public bathroom. A group of men in uniform talking about fishing stopped and stared at them for a long minute. Then a woman kindly took them behind the desk.

There was the weeping icon in a monastery on a dusty hill where the women had to choose wrap-around skirts and head-scarves from a big box by the door before they could be ushered into the chapel.

There was the time they saw two teenage girls ride bareback into town, leaving their horses untethered behind the dry goods store while they got ice cream cones.

The day-tripping had struck other people's fancy too. There was a day trips column in the weekly entertainment paper. There were local travel books to take along to help recall the name of the fabulous barbeque place with the great pork chops or the authentic Mexican cantina tucked away on a side street. The *New York Times* had started a weekly section of the paper called "escapes."

But the two women's traipsing seemed intensely private, and special. Its concrete pleasures and compulsions held the dream of being "in" a life—its rhythms, its stopping to contemplate still lifes. They could rest their eyes on the scenes they happened into. They would pick up little tidbits to bring home: Czech pastries, some peanut brittle, a butter dish in the shape of a sleeping cat. Cabins covered in creeping vines took on the solid ephemerality of an inhabited place. Local characters flickered in and out of view like dream figures. The women would drift into a feeling of possibility and rest.

It was certainly not small-town values or clean living they were after, but rather the way that the synesthetic web of fabulated sights and tastes made scenes and objects resonate. It was as if they could dwell in the ongoing vibrancy of the ordinary, leaving out the dullness and possible darkness.

The imaginary still lifes they carried home from their forays held the simple but profound promise of contact.

And the charged particularity of the objects, images, and events encountered framed the importance of making implicit things matter.

POTENTIAL

The potential stored in ordinary things is a network of transfers and relays.

Fleeting and amorphous, it lives as a residue or resonance in an emergent assemblage of disparate forms and realms of life.

Yet it can be as palpable as a physical trace.

Potentiality is a thing immanent to fragments of sensory experience and dreams of presence. A layer, or layering to the ordinary, it engenders attachments or systems of investment in the unfolding of things.

TRACES

People are collecting found objects snatched off the literal or metaphorical side of the road. Things that have dropped out of the loop or have been left sagging somewhere are dragged home as if they are the literal residues of past dreaming practices.

The snatching practice mixes a longing for a real world (or something) with the consumer's little dream of spying a gem or tripping over a bargain. And in the mix, all kinds of other things are happening too.

Andrew, out scavenging the neighborhood, finds a letter written in 1914 by an old woman to her nephew going to medical school. It's like a letter in a bottle. A curiosity piece. People like to look at it and hold its yellowed stationary in their hands.

> Sunday 22nd dawned dazzlingly fair but still too cold for comfort. However, I braved the blast to give a birthday greeting to a friend—a Dutch woman born in Holland, whose cake blazed with one hundred candles. I took as a little offering a pretty birthday card and a box of orange blossoms. The beautiful sprays were cut from two trees of the Louisiana orange I bought and my daughter Faith and I planted ourselves three years ago. The cold seems not to have touched them and I learn that this tree will live and thrive in a temperature of eighteen degrees. Well, the lady in attendance on the sweet centenarian selected a tiny wreath of the fragrant white buds and blossoms nestling in the glossy green leaves, and pinned it on the black silk cap of the old, old lady. The room was crowded—everyone applauded and the recipient was charmed. The first orange blossoms she had worn since her young girlhood's marriage.
>
> I trust all this doesn't bore your majesty—crowned with the weighty and mighty honor of twenty-one years! I'm glad you have to work—a boy is gravely handicapped who has a well-filled purse. God speed you to a true and worthy success! No matter if I do believe that work—honorable work—is the salt that savors life, had I money I'd fill your purse, I would. As it is—keep your dawn unsullied—and work for your purpose.

The strangely vibrant rhetoric of the letter makes it a "something" in itself, as if it could embody the conventions of a past time and yet also defy capture.

Her neighbor advertises his moving sale in the paper. He's got quality items: a new couch, oak bookshelves, and major appliances. By seven AM a hundred people are gathered outside the gates. It's a tense and strangely vital scene as strangers, bent on getting stuff, half bond and half vie for the best place to rush the gates when they open. One man goes and gets coffee and donuts to share. A woman and her daughter strategize about how to reach before anyone else both the media console sitting at the far end of the yard and the washing machine propped up on a dolly in the driveway. A grandmother is a habitual yard-saler. She laughs about how it got so bad she had to buy a pickup truck and build a second garage to store all the stuff.

Now bodies begin to maneuver and align. When the gates open at eight they rush in. By ten, everything has been carted away.

23

Ordinary scenes can tempt the passerby with the promise of a story let out of the bag.

Matter can shimmer with undetermined potential and the weight of received meaning.

One day she's walking through the gated communities of Irvine, California (where, as some who can't afford to live there, say, "All the trash cans sit on doilies and all the weeds grow in perfect rows"). She comes across a late-model, fire-engine-red Ford sedan parked at the curb on a cul-de-sac. Sprawled across the driver's door are the words "PMS POWERED." A snazzy car with an in-your-face attitude, it back talks the social snickering of PMS jokes.

She imagines the car driving around town as the moving scene of an attitude adjustment.

But when she walks around the car, she sees that both tires on that side are missing. The car is actually listing on one hastily placed jack left either by thieves in a hurry or by the harried car-owner in the middle of a compound problem. Now the car becomes another kind of thing. More complicated. Perched on the unpredictable or unimagined edge of the ordinary, it takes on the full charge of potential's two twisted poles—up or down, one thing or another. It sparks in the tension between drudgery and routine—the barely holding on—and the flash of event.

FIRST IMPRESSIONS

She's driving across the Texas Panhandle with a friend. A hotel rises up out of the cotton fields like a mirage in the middle of nowhere. They stop for the night. There is only the hotel, a gas station, and a truck stop surrounded by fields and highways as far as you can see.

They float in the big family pool in the lobby atrium. It's full of exotic plants. Two stairways cascade down from the balconies on the second and third floors. A few people are eating in the restaurant. The bar on the second floor is empty. The scene is a little flat, dead, not quite right. It's like an imitation mall in a place where mall culture has not quite taken off yet, even though the whole thing looks so five minutes ago relative to more urban-suburban-exurban places. It's like a partially realized (or, in other words, failed) miracle. A fantasy tentacle floating in the stormy placidity of the nowhere of dully compelling force peppered by dreams of getting out or *something*.

They walk across the street to the Rip Griffin truck stop. Half a dozen old men are sitting at the counter telling stories, bragging, and making public performances out of teasing each other. She imagines their homes in a small town somewhere out of sight across the fields, and how they must come to sit in this place because it's connected to "the road" and the real and imagined modes of traveling that ride its back. The scene has the moving stillness of an apparition of some kind of life marked as southern, or western, or rural, or small town, or ranch, or something.

As the two women walk in, the old men turn to look, stopping in mid sentence. They hold the silent stare for what seems to her like a shockingly long time. Then they return to their business but they keep shooting looks back at them, obviously aware not so much of having an audience, she thinks, as of having some kind of potential to plumb from the scene of the two women traveling together. As if strangers entering from the highway bring something with them. Or at least "strange" strangers in the middle of some kind of situation or event.

A few years later, she stops again. The truck stop has become a shiny yellow mini mall with a Pizza Hut, a Burger King, and a southern fast food place called Grandy's. It stinks of plastic. The old men have migrated to the hotel restaurant, which is now full of people and loud with banter. Everyone is smoking. There's only a tiny nonsmoking section tucked away in an isolated corner.

The hotel pool is closed to guests because there's a wedding. On the way back to her room, she stops to watch. The bride descends the open stairway. The pool has been decorated with tea lights, so it takes on the glamorous glow of a mini Taj Mahal. The men in the wedding party all wear black cowboy hats and boots, black jeans, and white shirts. The ceremony is brief and the reception that follows consists of sheet cake, potluck dinner, and nonalcoholic drinks. It seems unbelievably subdued for a wedding.

When she returns one last time a few years later, the hotel looks old and rundown. Her room smells of smoke and mold. The restaurant has closed. The hotel manager says it's too bad but they just can't keep good help. "They go back on welfare."

She crosses the street to the truck stop where an industrious young woman in uniform is washing the floors in the yellow food court. The young woman takes the trouble to ask the cook at the Grandy's to make another steak even though it's technically closing time.

She reads the local paper as she eats. A man is found not guilty by reason of insanity in his dad's murder. Turns out he's been having auditory and visual hallucinations for more than twenty years. A bridge has collapsed and divers have recovered more bodies from the river. There has been a head-on collision of two trains. No one knows how the two trains got on the same track. A bolt of lightning has killed a twelve-year-old boy. A few of the high school graduates are receiving small scholarships of $200 or $300, there are winning lottery numbers, the author of the Nancy Drew detective series dies at ninety-six, the authorities say it was a feud that led to the slaying of a South Texas man who had been shot and dragged by his ankles several blocks behind a pick-up truck. Two men are arrested for stealing street signs after the police receive a tip, a man reports someone putting water in the gas tank of his vehicle, a woman reports subjects dumping dead animals and trash in two vacant lots, two gas station clerks report gas drive-offs in the amounts of $9.30 and $3.00.

As she leaves, she reads the community bulletin boards by the door. There are people looking for odd jobs. There are ads for exercise classes, diet pills ("I lost 40 pounds in three months!"). There are a lot of ads for used cars ('84 Lincoln Continental, fully loaded). There are public service announcements for low-income services, a domestic abuse hotline, and the Texas runaway hotline. There are pictures of missing children. There are legal ads ("traffic ticket problems?"), church ads (Full Gospel Holy Temple Broadcast of Deliverance), ads for medical insurance, and baseball schedules.

These are only glimpses of a public culture shifting over time. Partial scenes saturated with expectations, impressions too easily gathered into a narrative of social decline (or whatever). These floating images do not begin to approach what might be happening to the ordinary in this time or place. It's just that the images strike her, seem to unfold into a puzzle's pieces or to promise some direct line into what's happening somewhere—in some place, this little corner in the cotton fields. You could say, of course, that the images that strike her in passing hide as much as they reveal. But you could also say they mean only exactly what they say—Look at this! Imagine that! Things happen! Here's something that might be for you! It's the paying attention that matters—a kind of attention immersed in the forms of the ordinary but noticing things too.

By now, Rip Griffin has a Web site with the headline "A family owned and operated business." It's a corporate myth with meanings that flash. "Since the early days of the Pony Express rider . . . evolved into modern travel centers . . . Rip Griffin . . . started his corporation with a one-pump gasoline station . . . it has since grown to a $250 million company . . . with Truck and Travel Centers in Texas, New Mexico, Colorado, California, Arizona, Wyoming and Arkansas." But no one who enters the truck stop for a coke or a meal cares about the Web site or corporate meanings per se.

THE "WE" OF MAINSTREAM BANALITY

A world of shared banalities can be a basis of sociality, or an exhausting undertow, or just something to do. It can pop up as a picture of staged perfection, as a momentary recognition, or as a sense of shock or relief at being "in" something with others.

A weirdly floating "we" snaps into a blurry focus when one enters a mall, or when one is flipping through reality TV channels, watching scenes unfold: the simulated thunderstorms tacked onto the national map on the weather channel; the bedroom transformed into an exotic dream room on the extreme-makeover shows; or the meal made like magic on the cooking channel.

The animate surface of ordinary affects rests its laurels in the banality of built environments and corporate clichés.

The "we" incites participation and takes on a life of its own, even reflecting its own presence.[8] It's a thing that happens when e-mails with joking commentary show up in your in-box and you pass them on for some reason. Or when intimate public slogans float into a collective mode of address: "Know what I'm sayin'?" "That's just wrong," "I don't THINK so," "That's what I'm talkin' about," "I hear you," "It's all good." Or when bumper stickers talk back to each other as if they can't help it: "Shit happens," "Magic happens," "My child is an honor student," "My child beat up your honor student," "Just say no," "Just do it," "Vote Bush," "I voted for Bush and got Dick," "Bush is a punk ass chump," "Bush bin Lyin'."

HARDWIRED

We take our cues so directly from circulating forces that the term "hardwired" has become shorthand for the state of things.

Little undulations are felt as pleasures and warning signs, as intoxications and repetitions in daily routine.

DRYER SHEETS

Weirdly collective sensibilities seem to pulse in plain sight.

A woman shows up at her door in the middle of the afternoon.

[8] See Michael Warner, *Publics and Counterpublics* (New York: Zone Books, 1997).

She and her husband are thinking of buying the big house across the street. She wants to know if anyone in the neighborhood uses chemicals on their lawns, or if anyone uses dryer sheets.

At first, she has to ask the woman what a dryer sheet is. But then images pop into her head: the sweet smell of dryer sheets coming in with the breeze on a cloudless day, the bright blue sky and the flowers in the yards, the little orange flags sticking up out of the grass at the schoolyard, warning that chemicals have been sprayed, the ChemLawn trucks parked up on widows' hill in front of the places with the big lawns.

She mutters a shorthand version of these things to the woman standing at her door, but really all it takes is a look and the woman is gone, leaving little seeds of anxiety to sprout.

THE PULL OF THE ORDINARY

The ordinary throws itself together out of forms, flows, powers, pleasures, encounters, distractions, drudgery, denials, practical solutions, shape-shifting forms of violence, daydreams, and opportunities lost or found.

Or it falters, fails.

But either way we feel its pull.

"JULY MOUNTAIN"

In "July Mountain," Wallace Stevens describes the poetics of an incipient universe.

> We live in a constellation
> Of patches and pitches,
> Not in a single world . . .
> The way, when we climb a mountain,
> Vermont throws itself together.

The "Vermont" that throws itself together in a moment is already there as potential. In other words, it's already problematized; already a question and a something waiting to happen. It exists in the differences and repetitions of a grab bag of qualities and technologies that can be thrown together into an event and a sensation. It is a potential mapping of disparate and incommensurate qualities that do not simply "add up" but instead link complexly, in difference and through sheer repetition and not through the enclosures of identity, similarity, or meaning, or through the logic of code. It is fall colors, maple syrup, tourist brochures, calendars, snow, country stores; liberalism and yet the fight over gay marriage; racial homogeneity and yet everywhere white lesbian couples with babies of color; the influx of New York wealth long ago rushing in to shore up that certain look of rolling hills and red barns and yet also the legacy of the dairy industry written onto the landscape and property laws; and the quirkiness, quaintness, dullness, and/or violence of village life in this time and place. The question is not where, exactly, this Vermontness came from — its "social construction," strictly speaking — but the moment when a list of incommensurate yet mapped elements throws itself together into something. Again. One time among many. An event erupting out of a series of connections expressing the abstract idea — Vermontness — through a fast sensory relay. Disparate things come together differently in each instance, and yet the repetition itself leaves a residue like a track or a habit — the making of a live cliché.

FIRST DATE

She stops in at a café on a town square in Ohio.

Two middle-aged people sit awkwardly together at the next table. A thin, blonde, carefully tanned woman is having a grapefruit while the heavy-set, pasty man is eating biscuits and gravy.

It's an odd scene—clearly their first meeting. The woman is talking about her workout schedule and what she eats. She says she's not obsessive about it but she likes to keep her body in shape. She pulls out bottles of vitamins and herbal supplements. "I take two of these when I wake up, these are with meals, these in the afternoon. These are good for energy if I feel a little low." She takes out lotions and rubs them into her skin.

He maintains a careful look of interest. But things don't seem to be going well for him.

A few minutes later she hears the grapefruit woman say to the biscuit man, "Of course, you'd have to lose thirty pounds." He's nodding. "Of course, oh yes." He's looking down at his biscuits and gravy. His eyes wander around the table at a level well below the range of possible eye contact. Then he lowers his head over his plate and eats.

She wonders how these two people found each other. This is before Internet dating, so maybe they used personal ads in the local newspaper. Maybe they were the only two single, middle-aged people in the county. Whatever it was, it was an experiment. Just to see what would happen. And things were happening, all right, even though "it" was so "not happening."

COLOR THERAPY

Face-to-face interactions and common encounters jump in a quick relay to floating sensibilities and the conditions of connection that link us.

In Las Vegas in the late 1980s, a post office outpost shares an ad hoc storefront with a flower shop and a gift shop sparsely filled with eclectic inexpensive ceramics. At noon, when the post office and store are closed for lunch, a color therapy group sometimes uses the space.

In one meeting a dozen people sit in a circle on gray-metal

folding chairs. One man is talking about a relationship problem that has something to do with the fact that he's a magenta. The people in the group respond with intricate discussions of the shades of color and color combinations that connect different personal energies and styles. Then a young woman begins to talk about a problem at work that stems from her being a yellow.

Now alternative health practitioners and mystics advertise color therapy on the Web. They use colored gemstones, candles, wands, prisms, light bulbs, water, fabrics, bath treatments, and eyewear to balance the body's energy and stimulate healing. Each color has a vibrational frequency; warm colors are stimulating; cool colors are calming; a strong attraction to certain colors might signal a particular imbalance.

You can play a game with color codes if you want to. Red is active, daring, passionate, and optimistic. Red people are courageous, confident, humanistic, strong-willed, spontaneous, honest, and extroverted. Purple is grand, idealistic, and sensitive, but may lack self-criticism and maturity. Purple people make good inspirational leaders. They are kindly and just, humanitarian, self-sacrificing, visionary, creative, and strong mentally. Magenta is less aggressive and more spiritual than red and also more practical than purple. Yellow is intellectual and communicative. Yellow people are good-humored, optimistic, confident, practical, and intellectual.

You can imagine yourself through the model of one of the types. Or against it. Maybe you'd like to be orange. Orange is more ambitious and self-sufficient than red, but lacks its warmth. It has the intelligence of yellow without its loftiness. Orange people are enthusiastic, happy, sociable, energetic, sporty, self-assured, and constructive. But then you might think you're actually probably closer to a green. And that's on a good day. Green is healing, sympathetic, steadfast, and restrained. Green people are understanding, self-controlled, adaptable, sympathetic, compassionate, humble, generous, nature loving, and romantic. You might begin to piece together combinations of colors and blends, making things up.

But the people who are really into color therapy don't read colors as symbols or codes. They're into the real surface qualities of colors and what they can do. They don't care what colors "mean." They're fooling around with the forces that be, to see what things are made of. They want to set things in alchemical motion. They're talking things over with like-minded people. You never know.

JUST DO IT

Meanwhile, down the street, at practically the very same moment that the color therapy group is meeting in the post office, a chemical factory explodes and blows up half the town of Henderson, Nevada.

The FEMA hearings drag on for months. There is testimony. Small businesses have been ruined by the blast. Unmarked trains carrying dangerous chemicals have been running along the edges of backyards where innocent children play. There's talk of secret big business operations supported by the federal government and of callous disregard for future generations.

She starts talking with the de facto leader of the small business owners. He feels slighted by FEMA. He and the others have confrontations with local politicians. There are sinister threats. There are fights. They're digging for dirt and finding plenty. Bob is devoting his life to the cause. He spends hundreds of dollars on long distance phone calls every month. He organizes a campaign to unearth stories: the young man who was raising tarantulas and poisonous snakes in his apartment to pay for college and lost everything in the blast; the retired couple who came to the town looking for peace or something and who awoke that night to the sound of windows and glass doors smashing all over the house and the smell of gas.

When Bob and the other small business owners get no satisfaction from the government, they decide to take things into their own hands. They come up with an idea to start over by building a chemical factory of their own. They already know plenty about manufacturing. This is America and they can do anything. Someone says he knows an engineer who'll work with them. Now they just need someone who knows something about chemicals.

Things keep getting worse. Bob is calling her every night. Then he's piecing together a conspiracy too big to talk about over the phone. She meets him in a church parking lot on the edge of town. The sunset is spectacular. Bob wants to tell her his life story: the big, beautiful, wild Nevada of his childhood; hunting and fishing in a pure land; his return, years later, to start his own business and raise his children right; then the explosion, just when he was beginning to get on his feet again. Now there are days he just wants to end it all. He takes his son fishing up at the lake and they're floating in a pristine scene. He has his gun with him and he's going to blow his head off. Because he's the kind of guy who, if he comes to the bottom of a mountain, he climbs it, straight up, no problem, that's just who he *is*. But the system is throwing up roadblocks in front of him so he can't even get to the mountain to dig his heels in and start working.

It's getting dark. He's talking too much about himself. She says she's talked to other people who have experiences like his and think the way he does. This makes him mad (much to her surprise). He's an individual. There's no one in the world like him. He isn't *like* anything. He comes on to her. She gets out of there but now she's anxious and her stomach is queasy. He keeps calling. She visits him once more—this time at his house with his wife and children. There's no furniture left in the house. They sit on the carpet in the empty living room and eat pizza out of the box. Everyone's very quiet. It's scary and depressing; there's something just a little bit "off" and terribly wrong. Now he's mumbling bitterly about things she can't quite hear and then she half realizes his talk has become lewd and is directed at her. This can't be happening. The air goes out of the room. She stands up and starts moving toward the door. She thanks his now wide-eyed wife. She leaves the house. He calls only once more, a couple of days later, to report on the progress of his case with FEMA. She's cool with him on the phone, not encouraging him to keep in touch. Keeping her distance (too late).

SCANNING

Watching and waiting has become a sensory habit.

She's no different from anyone else. All her life she's been yelling "Pay attention!" but now she's not so sure that's such a good idea.

Hypervigilance has taken root. There are the obsessive compulsives who keep close track of everything because they have to. Like the guy she heard about on the radio who spends his whole life recording everything he does. "Got up at 6:30 AM, still dark, splashed cold water on my face, brushed my teeth, 6:40 went to the bathroom, 6:45 made tea, birds started in at 6:53 . . ."

Or there are those like the neighbor on a little lake in Michigan where she and two other anthropologists live in a row of little houses. The neighbor's hobby is video taping every move he makes: his walks in the woods, his rides in his Model T Ford, his forays into Polish folk dances where old women go round and round the dance floor together, the monthly spaghetti suppers at the Catholic church in town. One night when the three anthropologists are gathered at one of their houses he stops by to give them a video of himself walking around the lake in the winter snow and ice. (At the same time he also gives them an xxx-rated porn video without explanation. Then he just leaves, saying he hopes they have a nice evening.) After dinner, they settle down to watch his home video. They hear his every breath and footstep. There are some deer droppings on the path and some snow piles that have suspicious shapes. Then he's walking up to Bob and Alice's cabin (they're in Florida for the winter) and he's zooming in on a massive lump pushing out the black plastic wrapped around the base of the house. Uh-oh. Could be ice from a broken water main. Maybe the whole house is full of ice. He wonders what will happen when the (possible) ice thaws. Could be a real problem. He says maybe he'll send a copy of his video to Bob and Alice down in Florida. Then he moves on. Back to the breathing, the icicles, the footsteps in the snow. Things are (potentially) happening and he is in the habit of paying strict visual attention. But he is not necessarily in the habit of getting to the bottom of things or of making a decision or a judgment about what to do. He is making a record of his own ordinary attention to things and it's this—the record of his attention—that he shares, indiscriminately, with the anthropologists gathered next door and maybe with poor Bob and Alice down in Florida. Possibilities and threats that pop up in the process remain lodged in the actual look of things and are preserved as such. He's an extremist, pushing things for some reason, but the close, recorded attention to what happens and to the intense materiality of things make some kind of sense to a lot of people and not just when they're watching *America's Funniest Home Videos* or reality TV.

There are those who give shape to their everyday by mining it for something different or special. Like her friends, Joyce and Bob, who live in the woods in New Hampshire. He is a lumberjack. She cleans the little 1950s tourist cabins with names like Swiss Village and Shangri-La. Joyce left her husband and four kids after years of living straight in a regime of beatings under the sign of Jesus. She went out the back window one day and never looked back. Then she met Bob when she was tending bar and they took a walk on the wild side together that lasted for a dozen happy years (though not without trouble, and plenty of it). She let him have his drinking problem because he worked hard. He would hit the bottle when he got home at night and all weekend long. She called him Daddy even though she was a good ten years older and pushing fifty.

They moved from rental cabin to rental cabin in the north woods. They invited raccoons into their cabin as if they were pets. They got up at 5 AM to write in their diaries. When they got home at night they would read their daily entries out loud and look at the artsy pictures Bob took of treetops and bee nests. Finally, they were able to get a low-income loan to buy a little fixer-upper they had found in some godforsaken place on the north side of the lake.

But then a card came from Joyce that said Bob had left her for "that floozy" he met in a bar.

She wonders if Joyce still keeps a diary, if she still fancies the serendipitous discovery of happiness and looks for ways to deposit it in the ordinary, or if something else has happened to her ordinary.

THE ANTHROPOLOGISTS

The anthropologists keep doing the fun things they do together, poking around. They knock on the doors of the little fishermen's huts on the frozen lake. They invite themselves in for a visit and sit down on the bench inside. But the fishermen don't say a thing. Not even "Who are you?" or "What are you doing here?" So they sit together in a wild, awkward silence staring down through the hole in the ice to the deep, dark waters below. They can't think of a single question that makes any sense at all.

When they take walks in the woods, they come across hunters. They are more talkative than the ice fishermen. They want the anthropologists to know that they aren't "Bambi killers." Maybe some other hunters are, but not them, the new breed. They're nice. They've been to college and have things to say about politics and the environment and the state. Most of the time there's a woman in the group. They're teaching her to hunt.

The game wardens are the bad guys. Everyone cowers when they come around a bend looking for poachers. They drive post-apocalyptic cars with burned paint that have been specially outfitted with giant guns and spotlights mounted on the hood. Rogue, mean-looking guys, they fix hard stares on you and you can see the muscles jump under their camouflage suits. These guys are jumpy.

THE JUMP

In Austin, joggers passing over the high bridge on the river stop to stretch their hamstrings on the metal rails. The expansive scene from the bridge suspends elements together in a still life: fishermen sit upright in flat-bottomed boats; giant blue herons perch on drowned cottonwoods; limestone mansions on the cliffs above throw reflections halfway across the river. Crew boats glide silently over the water. A riverboat thrusts itself slowly up the river, dredging the hard mass of the water up and over its wheel.

At times, the bridge is a stage for human dramas of intimacy, rage, quiet desperation, or simple pleasure.

One morning a crude sign is taped to the railing. At the top of the sign, two names, ANGELA AND JERRY, are slashed through with big black Xs. Below the names, the sign reads: RELATION-SHIP DESTROYED, WITH MALICE, BY FEDERAL AGENTS & A.P.D. [Austin Police Department] FOR BELIEFS GUARANTEED UNDER U.S. CONSTITUTIONAL BILL OF RIGHTS. I MISS YOU ANGELA, JESSICA, & FURRY DOG REEF. It's signed ALWAYS, JERRY. Below the signature, the words YANKEE GIRL are encased in a pierced heart and the words PLEASE COME BACK are highlighted with a thick black border. At the bottom of the page, the sign continues:

ANGELA, JESSICA AND FURRY DOG REEF . . . I MISS YOU. MAY
GOD HAVE MERCY ON THE SOULS OF THE HATEFUL, VINDIC-
TIVE PEOPLE WHO CONSPIRED TO TAKE YOU FROM ME, AND
DID SO WITH SUCCESS. ANGELA, I WILL LOVE YOU ALWAYS
AND FOREVER. I MISS YOU BABE, JERRY. Then another pierced
heart memorializes YANKEE GIRL. On the ground beneath the
sign there is a shrine of yellow ribbons and a Sacred Heart of Jesus
votive candle with half-burned sticks of incense stuck into the
wax.

The sign is both cryptic and crystal clear. Its fury quivers in its
wavering letters. It does not ask to be interpreted, but heaves itself
at the world, slashing at it like the self-slashing of people who cut
themselves to feel alive. This is a poetics as common as it is striking. It's the kind of thing you see everyday in the graffiti written
on train trestles, or in the signs the homeless hold on the side of
the road, in the wild talk of AM radio talk shows, in road rage,
in letters to the editor, or in the barely contained resentments of
workplaces and intimate spaces.

This is the ordinary affect in the textured, roughened surface of
the everyday. It permeates politics of all kinds with the demand
that some kind of intimate public of onlookers recognize something in a space of shared impact.[9] If only for a minute.

People might be touched by it, or hardened to its obnoxious
demands. But either way, a charge passes through the body and
lingers for a little while as an irritation, confusion, judgment,
thrill, or musing. However it strikes us, its significance jumps.
Its visceral force keys a search to make sense of it, to incorporate
it into an order of meaning. But it lives first as an actual charge
immanent to acts and scenes—a relay.

[9] For a discussion of "intimate publics," see Lauren Berlant, *The
Queen of America Goes to Washington City: Essays on Sex and Citizenship*.
Durham, N.C.: Duke University Press, 1997.

Affects are not so much forms of signification, or units of knowledge, as they are expressions of ideas or problems performed as a kind of involuntary and powerful learning and participation. Alphonso Lingis noted the jump of affect in his description of touring a mine at the Arctic Circle: "The young miner who showed me the mine put out every cigarette he smoked on his hand, which was covered with scar tissue. Then I saw the other young miners all had the backs of their hands covered with scar tissue. . . . when my eye fell on them it flinched, seeing the burning cigarette being crushed and sensing the pain. . . . The eye does not read the meaning in a sign; it *jumps* from the mark to the pain and the burning cigarette, and then jumps to the fraternity signaled by the burning cigarettes."[10]

Here, the abstracted sign of collective identity—the scar tissue on the back of everyone's hands—not only retains its tie to the problems of sense and sociality but demonstrates, or proposes, an extreme trajectory. It shows where things can go, taking off in their own little worlds, when something throws itself together.

Ordinary affects highlight the question of the intimate impacts of forces in circulation. They're not exactly "personal" but they sure can pull the subject into places it didn't exactly "intend" to go.

[10] Alphonso Lingis, "The Society of Dismembered Body Parts," in *Deleuze and the Theatre of Philosophy*, ed. Constantin Boundas and Dorothea Olkowski (New York: Routledge, 1993), 296.

Positions are taken, habits loved and hated, dreams launched and wounded.

And just about everyone is part of the secret conspiracy of everyday life to get what you can out of it.

She thinks it's sort of like being a water bug, living on the surface tension of some kind of liquid. Seduced by the sense of an incipient vitality lodged in things, but keeping oneself afloat, too.

And nimble. If you're lucky.

GAMES OF SENSE

There are games you can play.

Like the game of noticing when the car up ahead in traffic is about to change lanes. Some people have developed a sixth sense about this. They can tell when a lane change is coming even if the driver isn't signaling or the car itself isn't surreptitiously leaning to the edge of the lane or acting nervous.

Or there's the game of trying to pick the quickest checkout lane in a glance. This one's harder. How fast is that cashier? Does that woman have coupons? That one looks like a check writer. That one looks like a talker. There are so many variables and contingencies. Even a brilliant choice can be instantly defeated by the dreaded price check or a register running out of tape. And once you've made your choice, you're stuck with it.

Stuck in a fast lane gone bad, you might start to feel a little desperate for something to do. But you can make a phone call, make a list in your head, get to work on your palm pilot. You can scan the surrounding bodies and tabloid headlines for a quick thrill or an inner smirk. Or you can just check *yourself* out with a copy of *House and Garden* or *Glamour* or *Esquire*. Picture-perfect scenes flash up and snap into sense. You can relax into the aura of tactile bodies, living rooms, and gardens jumping from fantasy to flesh and back again right before your eyes. The glossy images offer not so much a blueprint of how to look and live as the much more profound experience of watching images touch matter. The jump of things becoming sensate is what meaning has become.

BEING IN PUBLIC

Sensory games spread fast, animating the pleasures and compulsions of being attuned to some kind of a common world of banal yet unspoken, or even occulted, sensibilities.

Shifting forms of commonality and difference are wedged into daily interactions. There are hard lines of connection and disconnection and lighter, momentary affinities and differences. Little worlds proliferate around everything and anything at all: mall culture, car culture, subway culture, TV culture, shopping culture, all the teams and clubs and organizations (sports teams, dog breeding clubs, scrapbooking clubs, historical re-creation societies, homing pigeon societies, off-road vehicle users clubs, book clubs, collecting clubs, fan clubs, country clubs, professional organizations, walking clubs, home schooling groups, ethnic organizations, adoption groups, sex groups, writers groups, neighborhood hangouts, coffee drinkers), addictions of all kinds (drugs, alcohol, sex, overeating, undereating, cutting, kleptomania), diseases of all kinds, crimes, grief of all kinds, mistakes, wacky ideas. There are scenes of shared experience—of tourists, or of locals versus newcomers, or of people of color walking on a white street, or of people waiting all day at the food stamp office. There are common attachments to musical genres or to dreams of early retirement.

But everyone knows there's something not quite right.

Stress is the lingua franca of the day. It can be the badge you wear that shows that you're afloat and part of what's happening— busy, multitasking, in the know. Or it can be a visceral complaint against being overworked, underpaid, abandoned by the medical system, or subject to constant racist undertows.

Stress can motivate you, or it can puncture you, leaving you alone in times of exhaustion, claustrophobia, resentment, and ambient fear.

It can tell the story of inclusion or exclusion, mainstreaming or marginality. But its widespread power to articulate something stems not from a meaning it harbors inside but from its actual circulations through forces and trajectories of all kinds: self-help culture, the power of the drug industry and direct advertising, social indifference, political depression, road rage, or the proliferation of countless intricately detailed little worlds built around major social injuries or inventive forms of recreation or reaction.

Stress is a transpersonal bodily state that registers intensities.

A thing like stress can linger and do real damage. Or it can also flow out of a household like water down the drain, as when someone who has been unemployed for far too long finally gets a job. Any job.

NOT EXACTLY NEW

This kind of thing is not exactly new.

Tom Lutz's *American Nervousness, 1903: An Anecdotal History* traces how neurasthenia, or "nerve weakness," snapped into place at the beginning of the twentieth century as a widely experienced mix of symptoms—insomnia, lethargy, depression, hypochondria, hysteria, hot and cold flashes, asthma, hay fever, "sick headache," and "brain collapse." Lutz describes the phenomenon as the embodied sensibility of an excitable subject adrift in a world of large-scale modernist social transformations. He also describes it as an unsteady and fraught structure of feeling that mixed a gothic imaginary of hidden threats and unseen forces with the optimism of the new consumerist-therapeutic ethos of self-realization, personal magnetism, and corporate charisma. Its hegemony spread not through the power of a master narrative to gather up widely disparate identities and conditions of life but because it literally articulated competing and conflicting forces of science, technology and medicine, religion and ethics, psychoanalysis, gender and sexuality, health and disease, class and race, art and politics.

Like stress now, it was a weird super-sign of difference turned on the body. And like stress now it could only be seen through its singularities: it had to be told as an anecdotal history in order to see how its elements kept throwing themselves together through difference and event.

ROGUE INTENSITIES

Rogue intensities roam the streets of the ordinary.

There are all the lived, yet unassimilated, impacts of things, all the fragments of experience left hanging.

Everything left unframed by the stories of what makes a life pulses at the edges of things.

All the excesses and extra effects unwittingly propagated by plans and projects and routines of all kinds surge, experiment, and meander.

They pull things in their wake.

They incite truth claims, confusions, acceptance, endurance, tall tales, circuits of deadness and desire, dull or risky moves, and the most ordinary forms of watchfulness.

It's the 4th of July and the roads are gridlocked after the fireworks.

Her friend Danny and his girlfriend are stuck in traffic. Then they notice that the guy in the car in front of them is starting to lose it. He backs up as far as he can, touching their bumper, and then surges forward to the car in front of him. Then a big space opens in front of him. Danny and his girlfriend watch as the scene moves into slow motion. The guy pulls his car forward as far as he can and then puts it in reverse and floors it, ramming them hard. He pulls his car forward again and throws it into reverse. They look at each other and jump out of their car. He rams their car again, this time riding up right over the bumper and onto the hood. His wheels spin and smoke when he tries to dislodge his car and then he just sits there. Danny sees him reach for something on the floor of the car and imagines a gun. A traffic cop is now staring at the guy but he doesn't make a move toward him. Danny goes over and tells the cop about the something reached for on the floor. He points out that there are all kinds of people on the sidewalk. Danny sees the cop is afraid. Danny goes over and pulls the guy out of the car. He brings him over to the cop. The cop arrests him.

The cultural landscape vibrates with surface tensions spied or sensed.

She gets called to jury duty. A young African American man is facing five years minimum sentence for breaking and entering. At the jury selection, the lawyers ask a room of four hundred people if anyone has a problem with that. She says *she* does. She objects to automatic sentencing. She wants to know the circumstances. And not just dead circumstances, but the live events. She tells hypothetical stories of injustice (what if he was stealing a loaf of bread for his children?). The lawyers are dead bored and openly rude. After dismissing a few other objections, they focus their attention on the only four black people in the room, all women. They prompt them. They ask them questions. They listen carefully to the brief, dignified answers they get.

When the crowd is dismissed for the day, she falls into step on the sidewalk behind the four women. They're much more animated now. They're saying they have no problem with punishment. If this man did what they say he did, he should be punished. But it isn't their place to judge. That's the Lord's place. The next morning, the four women go up to talk to the judge. He dismisses them from the jury selection. Then the defendant's lawyers immediately enter a guilty plea. The man gets twenty-five years because it's a repeat offense. She's amazed at the whole thing.

Sunday mornings, homeless men line up for breakfast at the Jehovah's Witness church down the street. Men of all colors, but this is no utopia of racial mixing. They look hot, tired, sour, and out of place. Like stick figures of abjection and wildness, they come on buses or walk across town carrying all their belongings in dirty backpacks. Then they make the trek back again. You can tell they hate this particular moment in their week.

She knows a woman in her forties who has never married and lives alone. Her life is full of work, good friends, and family, all kinds of passions and forms of self-knowledge. But it's like there's no frame to announce that her life has begun. She knows this is ridiculous, but she swims against a constant undertow.

She hears of a suicide in the neighborhood. A man in his thirties who rented a cute little stone house with a great yard where there used to be parties (before he moved in). His girlfriend had just broken up with him. Then she got worried when she couldn't reach him. She asked his neighbor to go in and look. He had been hanging in the kitchen for days. His relatives came from around the state and loaded up his stuff on trucks. They were fighting over it as if that were all they cared about. They were looking for his motorcycle. They accused the girlfriend of stealing it. Then someone found it parked in a neighbor's front yard; someone must have put it there.

RELIEF

Unwanted intensities simmer up at the least provocation.

And then a tiny act of human kindness, or a moment of shared sardonic humor in public, can set things right again as if any sign of human contact releases an unwanted tension.

She pulls up to a tollbooth in New Hampshire. The attendant says the guy in the car in front of her has paid for the next car in line. That's her. It takes her a minute to process what she's hearing. Oh! They both gaze at the car up ahead pulling into traffic.

She and Ariana are out walking in the neighborhood: white woman, brown baby. Some teenagers pass them, scowling; brown boys dressed tough, showing attitude. But as they pass she hears one of the boys say to the others in a sweet boy's voice "Did you see that *cute* baby?"

She's driving onto campus early one morning. The pickup in front of her stops in the middle of the road to let an older, heavy-set woman cross the street. The woman scampers across, too fast. Then she looks back, first at the man and then all around, with a big smile, vaguely waving. Too grateful.

FANTASIES DRIFT

Little fantasies pop up. Like the one in the car ad where two hip young white people are driving through the streets of New Orleans listening to a pleasantly funky soundtrack. Suddenly they realize that the vital scene of African American street life outside the car has come into synch with the music inside. They look at each other and shrug their shoulders in the pleasure of a surprise event. It's unbelievable but they can take it in stride. Keep moving. They (or you, the viewer, or the couple form, or whiteness, or hipness, or something) are sutured to a pretty picture with surround sound. They can just drift for a while.

A sensory dream of seamless encounter floats over the currents of racial fear, rage, segregation, discrimination, violence, and exhaustion.

This is not just ideology but an event, however fleeting or insignificant it seems to be, and whatever purpose or underlying causes it can be slotted into.

It's one of the many little *some*things worth noting in the direct composition of the ordinary.

DISAPPEARING ACTS

Ecstatic little forms of disappearance have budded up. We dream the dream of a finished life. The dream job or the dream body settles into a perfect form.

Or we dream of the kind of magic that comes in a flash. The sweepstakes cameras appear at your door when you are still in your housedress, and big bunches of balloons in primary colors are released into the air. Or UFOs come in the night and lift you up in an out-of-this-world levitation trick.

Disappearance has always been the genius of the so-called masses. We are gifted dreamers of getting away from it all, giving capture the slip, if only by slipping into the cocoon of a blank surface.

Blankness has blanketed the country, spreading smoothly through the comfortable uniformity of theme parks and gated communities, and the sprawling new shopping meccas of big-box stores for every corner of life—home, pets, coffee, books, garden, bed and bath, pizza, tacos, hamburgers, toys, babies, office.

Banality is the vitality of the times. You can slip into any of the places where it's on display and check out for a while without ever feeling disconnected for a second.

MASTER PLANNED

Everyone knows there's something not quite right about suburban sprawl: the deserts of plywood spreading over hayfields; the kids getting fat eating potato chips in front of the TV; the creeping lure of the affordable dream house that comes in the same four basic plans no matter where you are.

But the houses are big, beautiful, white, more than you ever expected to have. More than you can resist. One day you walk into a model home. It feels like walking into a dream. Everything is set up for the perfect family: the boy's room, the girl's room, the baby's room all ready like they're saying "Come on, family, move in." It makes it look so easy. So over and done with.

She visits a master-planned community built on an empty plane outside of town. There's a fire station, a school, a police station, a day care, and a green belt with running paths. There are no trees around yet and the house siding is still unmarred plastic.

She stops at a convenience store built to look like a southern country store. The sales office next to it is a cute little bungalow. Two men wearing pressed shirts are playing horseshoes on the lawn. They wave at her, big smiles. They yell, "Hey, neighbor!" She realizes these guys must be the realtors staging a scene. But this is obvious. It's as if it's not nostalgia for a small town that is being offered but the fabulousness of the built environment itself. It's as if the value of the new and emergent—the up-and-coming mode of community itself—is embodied in a shared dream of finished surfaces. It's a game of living lite. A value that only goes so far. Maybe it's not only the dream house (the more-house-for-your-money) that people are after when they buy a house here, but also the move to be part of what's happening and to be part of the light inevitability of it all, too, the seamlessness.

The air is full of sneering stereotypes about gated communities. There are cartoons about it all over the place, like the one about the older couple sitting in their living room complaining that that dead body is still out there on the lawn next door. But the sneering at clichés of conformity and isolation doesn't really get at what's going on. There's also something more basic about how the dream world is desirable precisely because it only goes so far. And something about how that dream wants to be sutured to the moment when things snap together. It's like flexing one's watching and waiting muscles, keeping them limber. And it's just as attuned to the possibility that things will fall apart, the elements dissipating or recombining into something else. Not exactly "passive," it's hypervigilant and always building itself up to the intensity where action can become reaction.

RV FREEDOM

Three million retirees live in upscale RVs fully loaded with kitchens, bathrooms, marble countertops, and TVs front and back. Everything is built in, tucked away, clever. The retirees are mostly couples, mostly white. They wear matching T-shirts and have bumper stickers that read "Home is where you park it" or "On the road and off the record." For them, every day is a new beginning. If you don't like where you're at, you can just get in and drive away. They have pets and projects. They're history buffs. They visit war monuments and ghost towns or follow the Lewis and Clark Trail. Or they visit theme parks all over the country. Or hunt treasure with metal detectors or prospect for gold nuggets. They seek out beautiful scenery or little New England towns with gazebos.

They use the national Wal-Mart atlas of store locations to plan their itineraries. They sleep in Wal-Mart parking lots. After a hard day of driving, they can shop for whatever they need and then go back out to the parking lot to make supper. They buy gadgets like a walkie-talkie set so they can find each other in the store. They meet other RVers in the parking lot and tour their rigs. They know Wal-Mart is bad for Main Street but where would this country be without competition? They say social inequality is a fact of life— what can you do? Their biggest problem is the price of gas.[11]

MAINSTREAMING

The objects of mass desire enact the dream of sheer circulation itself—travel, instant communication, movies, catalogues, the lure of new lifestyles patched together from commodities gathered into scenes of a possible life.

The experience of being "in the mainstream" is a concrete sensory experience of literally being in tune with a "something" that's happening.

But nothing too heavy or sustained.

[11] See *This Is Nowhere* (Missoula, Mont.: High Plains Films, 2000).

It's being in tune without getting involved. A light contact zone that rests on a thin layer of shared public experiences.

A fantasy that life can be somehow seamless and that we're in the know, in the loop, not duped. That nothing will happen to us, and nothing we do will have real consequences—nothing that can't be fixed, anyway.

The experience of being "in the mainstream" is like a flotation device.

But its very surge to enter life lite leaves in its wake a vague sense of all the circuits that give things a charge.

HOME IS WHERE THE HEART IS

Home is where the heart is. You can get inside and slam the door. We dream of the big, beautiful, sensate commodity-to-live-in, the bathroom done in the textures of old stone and precious metals, a utopia of colorful decor. But the synaesthesia of being at home is always already afloat in the circuits of the prevailing public winds—privatization, sensible accumulation, family values, or some kind of identity or lifestyle or something.

The American dream takes the form of a still life: the little family stands beside the suv in the driveway, looking up, stock portfolios in hand, everything insured, payments up to date, yards kept trim and tended, fat-free diet under their belts, community watch systems in place. Martha Stewart offers advice on the finishing touches.

But then the little disappearing acts start coming up right in the middle of home's retreat, adding a different charge to things. There are times when it seems as if everything the heart drags home is peppered with a hint of addiction, aloneness, something rotten or worthless.

Horror stories leak in over the airwaves. Seemingly ordinary intimate spaces are revealed to be scenes of hidden corruption, catastrophe, isolation, and crime. There are children on welfare beaten to death in their homes between visits from the social worker; men who burst into their exgirlfriends' trailers, shooting them and their new lovers in their beds; bodies discovered only after the neighbors hear the dog barking in there for days on end. News of the weird feature stories like the one about the educated, middle-class couple who calmly goes away on vacation, leaving behind a hundred cats—some dead, some alive, wild ones living in the walls.

WHAT'S GOING ON IN THERE?

Sylvie's neighbor Tommy has been "into it" in his house at the bottom of the hill. He has a woman in there with him. She's a drinker. She sits in front of the tube and never sticks her head out. Sylvie has seen her down there drunk in the yard and the foulest language you've ever heard. One time it got so bad that Sylvie had to send Juanita down there to see about them. When Juanita got down there, Tommy had this woman handcuffed to the radiator and he was smashing her head against the floor. The police had to take him away. And then, of course, she went right back to him. Sylvie said you'd only have to beat up on her *once*. Juanita told Tommy and the woman she didn't care if they killed each other, she hoped they *did*, but they better not do it in front of Tommy's little girl. Juanita took the girl to stay with her up on the mountain until things settled down.

BLUE TV NIGHTS

In Las Vegas, she suspected that the guy next door was beating his family. She would hear fights at night through the thin walls of the trailer. He'd yell, something would go thud against the walls, the woman would scream, teenagers would skulk out of the trailer and hang around outside, despondent. Then one day the guy was having a cigarette on the little porch. The railing broke and he fell face down in the gravel expanse that serves as the yard. He lay there face down without moving. His wife and kids came out slowly, carefully; they peered at him from a good twenty yards away. "Are you ok?" Long pause. "No. I'M NOT OK." But they kept their distance, frozen in a vignette.

Not long after that, the family was gone. No moving vans or waves good-bye, just there one day and gone the next. Then she realized that the guy was still in there. One night she heard him laughing maniacally. Full beer cans thudded against the walls. After that, she began to notice the TV turned up loud at night, its blue light flashing in the darkened trailer, and him laughing loud at the wrong moments. One night she caught him standing at his living room window staring out at her. She got heavy curtains and kept them closed. Then she would notice the top of his head peering out of one of the three little window panels on his living room door. She pictured him standing on his tiptoes. She thought he must be completely deranged by now, if he hadn't always been. Every once in a while at night she would take a quick scan to see if the top of his head was there at the little window.

Years later, a friend living in Austin told her the same story. There was some weird guy next door in there alone after the woman left him. He was throwing beer cans against the walls in the dark and laughing at the wrong times to the flashing blue light of the TV.

THE TV REPAIRMAN

Her brother's cable is out. When the repairman arrives he says, "Do you know who I am?" It turns out that he's been on the news. He went into a house to repair a TV. He was down on his knees working when he was attacked by the family's pit bull. The dog had his jaws locked on the guy's leg and the family just laughed. Luckily, the guy had his tool belt on, so he grabbed a screwdriver and killed the dog. The dog's owners were outraged. But the repairman was a victim and a hero on the local news.

When she heard this story, she remembered an e-mail she got from an acquaintance who liked to send her stupid jokes and quirky stories:

> A homemaker's dishwasher quit working so she called a repairman. Since she had to go to work the next day, she told him, "I'll leave the key under the mat . . . Fix the dishwasher, leave the bill on the counter, and I'll mail you the check . . . By the way, don't worry about my Doberman . . . He won't bother you, but whatever you do, do NOT under ANY circumstances talk to my parrot!" When the repairman arrived at the homemaker's place the next day, he discovered the biggest and meanest looking Doberman he had ever seen . . . But just as she had said, the dog just lay there on the carpet, watching the repairmen go about his business . . . However, the parrot drove him nuts the whole time with his incessant yelling, cursing, and name-calling . . . Finally the repairman could not contain himself any longer and yelled, "Shut up, you stupid, ugly bird!!" The parrot replied, "GET HIM, Spike!"

55

COCOONS

Home is where the heart is. But take one foot out of the frame and things get sketchy fast. At the unwanted knock on the door, or the sudden ring of the phone at night, you can feel the uncanny resemblance between the dazed state of trauma and the cocooning we now call home.

The home cocoon lives in a vital state—open, emergent, vulnerable, and jumpy.

It lives as a practiced possibility, emergent in projects like home remodeling, shopping, straightening up the house, rearranging furniture, making lists, keeping a diary, daydreaming, or buying lottery tickets.

Practices that stage the jump from ideal to matter and back again can fuse a dream world to the world of ordinary things. Objects settle into scenes of life and stand as traces of a past still resonant in things; on a dresser top are loose change, pens, receipts, books, scattered jewelry, knickknacks, a kid's drawing, and a long-discarded list of urgent things to do. A small wooden table arranged by a window holds the promise of a profoundly secluded interior.

But the dream of approaching the ordinary lives only in the moment of its surge—in the resonance of the still life or the practice of the perfectly manicured lawn. Left to its own devices, it undoes itself through its own excesses. It drifts off in a flight of fancy, leaps into a wild plan of action, and overextends itself. It grows wild tendrils that harden into nodules of paranoia, perfectionism, or private dysfunction. It tries to fix itself into a code as if it could imprint itself on the world—like magic. In the gated community the rules of community order soon reach a tottering point open to parody and endless legal contestation: garage doors have to be kept shut at all times, drapes must be in neutral colors only, no digging in the yard without permission, no clotheslines in the yard, no pickup trucks in the driveway, no planting without permission, no grandchildren visiting in a senior compound. No exceptions.

THE TURNER DIARIES

The Turner Diaries is a racist, fascist novel from 1996 written under a pseudonym (Andrew MacDonald) by William Luther Pierce, the late leader of the National Alliance, a white separatist organization. The book is a prophesy of a new world order founded on racial genocide. The story begins with "the terrible day" in an invented past when government thugs broke into citizens' houses, tore apart seemingly solid walls to unearth hidden guns, and arrested hordes of people, rounding them up like cattle. This origin trauma incites a militia movement, which the book imagines through the details of a postapocalyptic "ordinary." It reads like a "how-to" manual for right wing conspiracy theorists and survivalists, and it has been credited with inspiring, in detail, the Oklahoma City bombing. Some also draw uncanny links between the description at the end of the book of a suicide mission to bomb the Pentagon and the actual attack that occurred on September 11, 2001. In the book, September 11 is also the date that "the Organization" carries out an assault on the city of Houston (and the date is also William Luther Pierce's birthday). Such is the world of strange and floating links that *The Turner Diaries* comes from.

But what is most surprising about the book is its focus on domestic scenes and the ordinary details of everyday life. The tips it offers are not just about how to organize armies and make bombs but also how to set up cozy shelters and keep house while living underground. The heroes distinguish themselves not by acts of bravery and camaraderie but by honing their skills in engineering, shooting, sexual performance, and housekeeping.

It's a recipe book for domestic competence.

A little world comes into view. It is a world based on a military model of community and skill, but it is one that is filled, too, with the textures and sensory details needed to imagine a dream world.

This lived, affective constellation of practices and sensibilities make the book not just an ideological diatribe (which it certainly is) but also a scene of life filled with worries, fetishes, compulsions, and hoped-for satisfactions.

It is possible to imagine how, for those readers who find it compelling but are not about to build bombs, it's a kind of self-help book. Self-help racism.

For the uninducted reader, on the other hand, reading it is an eerie experience haunted by what seem at first to be bizarre links between a racist rage at disorder, contamination, and decay and an appreciation for the well-tended suburban lawn, the Martha Stewart–inspired interest in interior design, and the fantasy game of reading catalogues to imagine oneself in that dress, with that face, or holding that particular gun.

THE SELF

The self is no match for all of this.

It's a dreamy, hovering, not-quite-there thing.

A fabulation that enfolds the intensities it finds itself in. It fashions itself out of movements and situations that are surprising, compelled by something new, or buried in layers of habit.

It can become hyperresponsive—touchy, volatile, and tuned in—or it can grow dull with anxiety. It gets caught in the quick, repetitive cycles of ups and downs—the flights of fancy followed by disappointments, satisfactions, rages, or dreams of rest.

It exists, obliquely, in dreams of disappearing, of winning or being done with it all. Forms of attention and attachment keep it moving: the hypervigilance, the denial, the distraction, the sensory games of all sorts, the vaguely felt promise that something is happening, the constant half-searching for an escape route.

BORDERLINES

Her friend Danny worked night shift on the suicide prevention hotline for a while. He said the borderline personalities were the worst. They kept calling back, looking for attention. He got to know them all, indulging them in their tiresome games and trying to help them if he could figure out when they were being straight. But then they would slip out of reach and then call back later, starting the cat-and-mouse game again.

But at exactly 4 AM all the calls would stop dead and he would lie down on the floor to sleep for the last two hours of his shift. He said he guessed even borderlines had to sleep *some*time. It was weird, though, how it was like clockwork.

THE AFFECTIVE SUBJECT

The affective subject is a collection of trajectories and circuits. You can recognize it through fragments of past moments glimpsed unsteadily in the light of the present like the flickering light of a candle. Or project it onto some kind of track to follow. Or inhabit it as a pattern you find yourself already caught up in (again) and there's nothing you can do about it now.

You can comfort it, like a child. Or punish it for getting off track, even for a minute.

Out there on its own, it seeks out scenes and little worlds to nudge it into being. It wants to be somebody. It tries to lighten up, to free itself, to learn to be itself, to lose itself.

None of this is easy. Straight talk about willpower and positive thinking claims that agency is just a matter of getting on track, as if all the messy business of real selves could be left behind like a bad habit or a hangover. But things are always backfiring. Self-making projects proliferate at exactly the same rate as the epidemics of addictions and the self-help shelves at the bookstore.

The figure of a beefed-up agency becomes a breeding ground for all kinds of strategies of complaint, self-destruction, flight, reinvention, redemption, and experimentation. As if everything rests on agency's shoulders. But there's always more to it than that.

ODD MOMENTS

At odd moments in the course of the day, you might raise your head in surprise or alarm at the uncanny sensation of a half-known influence.

The streets are littered with half-written signs of personal/public disasters. The daily sightings of the homeless haunt the solidity of things with the shock of something awful. They hold up signs while puppies play at their feet: "Hungry," "Will work for food," "God bless you." The sign hits the senses with a mesmerizing and repellent force. It pleads to be recognized, if only in passing. It gestures toward an ideological center that claims the value of will-power ("Will work for food") and it voices a simple dream of redemption ("God bless you"). But it's too sad. It offers no affect to mime, no scene of common desire, no line of vitality to follow, no intimate secret to plumb, no tips to imbibe for safety or good health.

There is no social recipe in circulation for what to do about homelessness, or even what to do with your eyes when confronted with it face to face.

The eye glances off the graphic lettering of the homeless sign as something to avoid like the plague. But the sign also prompts the surge of affect toward a profound scene.

A dollar bill stuck out of a car window gets a quick surge forward and the heightened, unassimilated, affect of a raw contact. "God bless you."

Things have started to float.

It's as if the solid ground has given way, leaving us hanging like tender cocoons suspended in a dream world. As if the conditions and possibilities of a life have themselves begun to float.

We notice our common drifting and the isolation and conformity in it. We know it's fueled as much by circuit overloads and meltdowns as by smooth sailing. But there's no denying that it has a buoyancy too. A vibrancy alive with gamblers, hoarders, addicts, and shopping malls.

61

GO HOME A HERO

We shop.

Sometimes, or all the time.

Too much or not enough.

With flare or with shame.

For necessities, for therapy, on vacation.

At Dollar Store or Neiman Marcus or Sears, depending.

We shop at the megastores because they're cheap and convenient and everywhere and because they're what's happening. Their weirdly upbeat slogans like "Getting It Together" and "Go Home a Hero" give shopping a slightly surreal charge. Day-glow orange pricing cards stick out at right angles from the shelves so you can't miss the sale items.

If you have plenty of disposable income, that's one thing. If you have no money at all, that's another thing.

If the money is tight, you're supposed to shop with mind-numbing, penny-pinching care. All those coupons. All those catalogs, the fantasies, the games of imagining having this thing or that and what you would do with it. Then the splurges on a tub of ice cream or the suicidal squandering of a trip to Las Vegas.

She shops with Ariana at supermarkets that play loud music. She runs up and down the aisles to make her laugh. People smile or come over and say something. One day a group of kids follow them around the store, bouncing in single file and making peek-a-boo faces for the baby. Another day a man next to them in an aisle starts making birdcalls. Ariana snaps her head to attention and stares at his mouth, amazed, while he runs through dozens of expert imitations.

One day in Walgreens she sees a handsome young man waiting in line. He wears a mechanic's uniform with his name stenciled on the pocket. When he talks or smiles he holds his hand up over his mouth but everyone stares anyway. His teeth are grossly misshapen. A few stick straight out of his mouth. There's a double row on one side. Like he's never been to a dentist—not as a child, not now.

Sometimes she shops at Foodland—a poor people's supermarket that everyone calls Food-stamps-land. The music is more raucous than at the other stores. It smells of disinfectant and the cashiers wear layers of thick gold chains around their necks or thick baby-blue eyeshadow. Homeless people walk up from the river for cheap beer and bread. People live in cars and vans in the parking lot. She begins to notice a woman who lives with her two kids in a truck. She has long, black hair and there's always a big circle of white on the crown of her head. One night there's a jumpy, red-faced man with her. He runs up to her, excited by his discovery that they have six-packs for two dollars. She gives him a hard stare. He says "What? Coke! I'm talking about coke! I found a good deal on coke for the kids!" He tries to act outraged, as if he thinks he's an unsung hero, but it's like he's not quite up for it.

A few days later, she sees the jumpy, red-faced man on campus. He's on foot, crossing the street at the entrance to campus with three other men—two Latinos and one African American. They are carrying big yellow street signs, and the red-faced guy is saying, "Isn't this great? What did I tell you? MAN!" They are moving fast, nervous and excited. But the minute they hit the campus sidewalk they hesitate, gathering in a loose circle. The black man says something about security . . . the cops. "What the fuck! Oh, SHIT!" A cop car pulls up to the curb in front of them. The black man bravely goes over and sticks his head in the window. Then the red-faced guy slowly sidles up to the car. They haven't been on campus more than sixty seconds.

(DIS)ORIENTATION

The ordinary can happen before the mind can think. Little experiences of shock, recognition, confusion, and déjà vu pepper the most ordinary practices and moves. Sometimes you have to pause to catch up with where you already are.

In Target the cashier asks her what the vacuum cleaner bags she's buying are for. "What?" She doesn't understand what she's asking. Maybe vacuum cleaner bags have gone defunct or something. The cashier says when *her* vacuum cleaner stops working she just throws it away. "What?" The cashier says she didn't know they made bags for vacuum cleaners. "What?" She thinks maybe they make disposable vacuum cleaners now, or something. Maybe that's what the young people use. Whatever. But she's a little alarmed. Or disoriented. Or something.

One day in PetSmart she has déjà vu. Her partner, Ronn, is talking to a clerk in front of the bank of fish tanks, while Ariana wanders from tank to tank, pressing her face up against the glass. There's a wall of aquamarine blue water with shimmering flecks of orange. She has the sensation that she's been in exactly this scene before, if only in a dream.

In the early 1990s a stapler built into a copy machine takes her aback. It's the last week of a fellowship at the Humanities Research Institute in Irvine. She's frantically copying journal articles to take home with her. One of the other research fellows walks in, sticks some papers into a slot on the side of the machine, and pulls them out stapled. She feels a slight shock at the discovery that copy machines now have staplers built into them. A sense of unease spreads through her in a tangle of thoughts. What else doesn't she know about? Why doesn't she hear about these things? She feels her mother's anxiety about answering machines, cell phones, self-serve gas pumps, and ATM machines. It's the fear of being caught up in something you can't master, of being found out. A kind of illiteracy.

She uses eBay to buy crib sheets and Teletubbie videos. One day she gets an e-mail with a colorful certificate of achievement. "Congratulations on your success! You're A Rising Star at eBay!" She's earned a yellow star for getting a good feedback rating from eBay sellers. She's a valued member of the eBay community. "Keep shooting for the stars!" She feels slightly depressed, or slightly stunned.

Her friend Andrew comes back to the neighborhood for a visit after being away for a year and a half. He says it's great to be back but unnerving ("Have I been away?"). So many things are the same, and then every once in a while there's something really different that comes as a shock, like a house all of a sudden where there used to be an empty lot or an open field. How did it get there? Who are those people inside, and how did they get the basketball trophies up on the wall so fast?

EXTREME TRAJECTORIES

Big social shifts float by on distant, cloudy discourses and scandals. The conditions of life assemble themselves into something and then morph into something else. Sometimes extreme trajectories take root and then take off with a life of their own.

Ian Hacking's *Rewriting the Soul: Multiple Personality and the Sciences of Memory* traces how the 1980s day care (sex abuse) scandals morphed into recovered memory syndrome and then into extreme trajectories like Multiple Personality Disorder (MPD) and Satanic Ritual Abuse (SRA).

Day care was (and is) a tense issue rooted in the conditions of work, gender, class, race, the family, and the state. One working mother had a drinking problem that led to a working problem that was articulated with the mass of public feelings about this situation—the guilt, the stress, the rage. Stories of child abuse and sexual abuse were beginning to circulate with force. Somehow her small child related a story of sexual abuse at day care and a dream world blossomed. Before we all woke up, there were court cases, convictions (all later overturned), kids pulled out of day care, women pulled out of work, male day care workers pulled out of the picture permanently.

Mass-market books and the popular movies they spawned provided the prototypes for the extreme trajectories of trauma and abuse. Then therapists helped their patients write the original multiple personality stories and suggested the disorder to other patients, asking them to identify with a compelling narrative of symptoms and causes. Talk shows spectacularized multiple personality disorder by showcasing victims with ever more elaborate presenting symptoms and more and more personalities. The standard quickly shifted from having sixteen personalities to having over a hundred, and the therapeutic aim shifted from one of trying to reintegrate the personalities to one of identifying and cataloging the "multiples."

Conflicts between believers and disbelievers, and between trauma culture and rationalism, also fueled the extreme trajectories of these movements. A professional couple whose daughter had recovered memories of child abuse founded the False Memory Syndrome Foundation—a highly focused and sophisticated pressure group that was eventually able to shift the blame from parents committing child abuse to therapists and their troubled patients producing an abuse hysteria. People with multiple personality disorder founded a society of their own that celebrated rather than pathologized their symptoms, thereby turning the "disorder" into a liberation movement. They began to use the term "alters," articulating with the diffuse New Age celebration of altered states of consciousness to experience spiritual energies. Rationalists attacked the "pseudoscience" of the movement as a symptomatic disease in itself. Strands of feminism promoting the recognition of child abuse contributed to counterattacks. Some therapists who had become activists for their patients accused skeptics of being a support group for child abusers.

Then even more extreme trajectories took off. Increasingly bizarre events were recalled and accusations took a strange turn into the highly scripted story of Satanic Ritual Abuse. A radical wing of the movement came to believe that patients suffering from dissociative disorders had been ritualistically abused by satanic cults run by their parents and featuring the bloody sacrifice of babies. Police and social workers developed elaborate lists and maps of the elements and scenes of Satanic Ritual Abuse, using them as diagnostic tools and standards of evidence in hundreds of court cases. The opposing side argued that the therapeutic movement itself had practices that were very much like cult initiation, including hypnosis and suggestion.

Such trajectories and metamorphoses are not just dead social constructions that we can track back to a simple origin, but forms of contagion, persuasion, and social worlding.

Flash mobs are leaderless gatherings organized by cell phone, e-mail, and the Web. The mobs usually do something silly, demonstrating only that a floating connection can flash into flesh.

At a Toys 'R Us, a flash mob stared at an animatronic Tyrannosaurus rex, and then fell to the floor with screams and waving of hands before quickly dispersing. In New York, participants assembled at the food court in Grand Central Station, where organizers (identifiable by the copies of the New York Review of Books they were holding) gave mobbers printed instructions regarding what to do next. Shortly after 7 PM about two hundred people suddenly assembled on the mezzanine of the Grand Hyatt Hotel next to Grand Central Station, applauded loudly for fifteen seconds, then left.

When Howard Dean was running for president, a Doonesbury comic strip called for a Howard Dean flash mob. Time: Saturday, September 13, 10:35 AM. Place: Foot of Space Needle. Activity: Link arms in an enormous circle, hop up and down chanting "The Doctor is in!" Disperse. The idea immediately appeared on Howard Dean's "Get Local" Web site as an action tool.

Another flash mob tried to produce a momentary supercomputer to compete with the fastest and most expensive computers in the world by bringing conventional computers to a single location, networking them together and putting them to work on a major scientific problem. It didn't work, but it almost did.

ERUPTIONS

Things flash up—little worlds, bad impulses, events alive with some kind of charge.

Sudden eruptions are fascinating beyond all reason, as if they're divining rods articulating something. But what?

SCENES OF IMPACT

Scenes of impact catch the senses: LA in flames, a trailer wrapped in crime scene tape, the memorial ribbons and stuffed animals lying at the feet of a still-smoking building. The plots become so familiar we can list them in shorthand: disgruntled workers going postal; jilted lovers and kids with guns opening fire in public; orderly men who keep too much to themselves revealed to be serial killers burying bodies in their backyards; the black men beaten, raped, and killed by cops; homegrown militias whipped into rage at the sight of unmarked helicopters and the stench of lost freedoms; messages coming through the mail as literal letter bombs or with anthrax in white powder or in a brown sandlike substance.

These scenes have an afterlife; it isn't like you can put a stop to them. Following the details of a breaking event is as compelling as doing a crossword puzzle; once you get into it you have to stick with it so you can get to the end and get out. One day there is the amazing scene of O. J. Simpson's white Ford Bronco traveling down an L.A. freeway, and before you know it you are into the glove, the blood stains, the barking dog, the racist words of the detective, the verdict, the reactions. Later, there are the sightings of O. J. playing golf in Florida and the sales of white Ford Broncos skyrocketing. We watch, amazed, as the Clinton-Lewinsky scandal spreads through a string of serial fetishes: the stained dress, the thong panties, the tapes, the neckties, the cigar. The details incite a sensory imagination that spirals off, following leads.

Scenes of public attention routinely drift over the fence of official news into eccentric circulation. Andrew Cunanan goes on a killing spree. After a few days of trying to track the traveling clues of his love life, his friendships, and his murders, the story flashes into a life of its own in multiple sightings of the actual man on the run. Someone spots him in Lebanon, New Hampshire, in a gray Mercedes Benz with Florida license plates and his pockets stuffed with money. The money is falling out of cracks and crevices in his clothes like a twisted fashion statement from the guy who killed the king of fashion. But all that turns out to be just apparitions or something. There is never any real effort to determine what, exactly, such things are.

WHATEVER

Jokes circulate about how we might as well just wire ourselves directly to sensation buttons and skip the step of content altogether.

One day, shortly after 9/11, she gets an e-mail from a friend in the neighborhood who likes to keep up a running commentary on quirky characters and scenes spied from her studio windows or fabricated on drowsy afternoon walks. Her friend writes:

> Here's a good story we would have had a few yuks about during coffee club. A friend of mine works @ St. Luke's Roosevelt hospital in a building that housed several psychology and psychiatry offices. Of course, it's not the big money area and the building is very rinky-

dink and tenement-ish, not a big target for anthrax, let's just put it that way. She works with mothers who have drug abuse problems, and the office downstairs treats juvie-delinquent adolescent types. Apparently, a few weeks ago one of the women who work in the office downstairs turns on the a/c (window unit) for a little conditioning action and a white dust sprays out all over her. Yikes! They call the Center for Disease Control and men in white suits and gas masks invade. My friend who is working upstairs is dubious—and so the people in her office just stay and work while the downstairs is cordoned off and investigated. They rush the substance off to the lab and put everyone who was in the office on Cipro. Then the test results come back. Low and behold, the substance tests positive for cocaine! So good, isn't it? They think one of the juvies hid their stash in the a/c when he was afraid of being searched. I think it's a brilliant idea to start pumping cocaine into the workplace. No need for caffeine anymore, let's just move right on up to the next level of productivity inspiration. Whadaya say?

SWARMING

We will follow any hint of energy, at least for a little while.

When something happens, we swarm toward it, gaze at it, sniff it, absorb its force, pour over its details, make fun of it, hide from it, spit it out, or develop a taste for it. We complain about the compulsion to participate. We deny its pull. We blame it on the suburbs and TV and ourselves. But we desire it too, and the cure is usually another kind of swarming, this time under the sign of redemption: a mobilization for justice, a neighborhood watch committee, some way of keeping our collective eyes open. Something to do.

She's living in a trailer park outside Nellis Air Force Base in Las Vegas. Her place is burglarized in plain daylight. Someone hurls a brick through a window, rifles through everything, steals a worthless old stereo, and sticks a note onto the living room wall with a large pair of scissors. The note says, simply, "Yeah, boy." She calls the police. "Kids," they say. They roam through the rooms looking at all the stuff pulled out of drawers, the computer unplugged and ready to go. She shows them the note stuck in the wall. Their eyes look at it and then drift over the walls, skimming the dozens of black-and-white photographs of weathered characters tacked up. "Did they stick these up too?" "No, those are mine." They look at her.

She calls the maintenance man to come fix the window. He can't get a piece of plywood until the next morning, so she carries her computer over to his trailer. His living room is empty. He tells her he came home the week before to find that his girlfriend had emptied the place and left, just like that. She took her three kids with her. And she took the only thing he had ever won — a five-piece blue velvet living room suite. He had built a playscape for the kids in the yard: a wooden bridge over a little plastic pool; rough, handmade chairs lined up against the trailer like the chairs of the three bears; a machine of some sort covered with stickers. He had been planning to get goldfish for the pond. Now the old girlfriend is calling him in the middle of the night to tell him how great the sex is with her new boyfriend, and one day he even went over to fix their toilet while they stood watching him.

Out of the blue he asks her to marry him since he's alone and she's alone. They could help each other. She says no thanks. The next day he helps her move to a single-wide trailer three streets over. He won't take any money so she takes him out to dinner. He wants to use a coupon a woman gave him in lieu of a day's pay for helping her move her office. He doesn't know where the place is, though, so she gets the name and address off the coupon. Dean's Roadside Café. She drives up and down a long road lined with strip malls. She asks him if he can see the place. "What letter does it start with?" She looks at him: "a D." Minutes pass. She asks him again if he can see it. He admits he doesn't know what a "D" looks like. She finds the place—a sport's bar—and they order sandwiches. Nervously, he gives the waitress the coupon and explains that someone gave it to him. The waitress stares at the little piece of paper, scowling. "What's this supposed to be?" "She said it was a coupon to get one free." "No, you can't use this here. It's been whited out." She looks at him like he's a criminal.

On the way home, they have to stop at a casino. He insists they use valet parking. Then he rushes in, changes a twenty dollar bill, and loses it in a slot machine in less than a minute. She can't believe how perfunctory it is—like blowing your nose or going to the bathroom or something. They leave immediately. He says he never brings more than twenty dollars.

A few days later he leaves on a midnight bus to Houston. He asks her if she knows where the bus station is and how he might get there. Then he's just gone. He doesn't say goodbye to anyone. He doesn't let his boss know he's leaving because he's afraid he'll be mad and won't let him go. She finds out the manager has only been paying him enough for some food and letting him stay in his trailer. Now he's off, looking for a life. He's got an old girlfriend in Houston. She's married now, so she's out, but her daughter had a crush on him when she was kid. She's a paraplegic now from a car wreck. He's hoping he can go there and take care of her and be her man. That's his plan. He sells everything he can to get a hundred dollars for a bus ticket. Somehow he gets himself to the bus station and he slips away. She never hears anything more about him.

The park manager calls a community meeting. He announces that all the break-ins are over. She points out that hers just happened. A line of bulky, stern-looking, air force guys leaning against the back wall of the Quonset hut shift their weight from one foot to the other. They murmur something about putting a stop to it once and for all. One of them catches her eye with a hard look she can't quite read.

Then people start noticing a late-model, brightly colored, party jeep patrolling up and down the streets at all hours of the night with its headlights off. One night, when she wakes up to the sound of it slowly passing, she looks out and sees the dark shapes of four or five men hanging off the sides of the jeep with semiautomatic guns and spotlights in their hands. It's as if some floating images of "community" and "action" have suddenly become visceral. As if they've been taken too literally, merging with the graphic repetitions of reality TV cop shows. As if "community" itself has drifted over some line into a state of free-fall, scripting the everyday with surreal scenes of strange community meetings and jeeps passing silently in the night.

She and some of the others have to call another emergency meeting to get these guys to stop before they shoot someone's teenager.

The soldiers do what they're told.

CLARITY

The nightly news reports an endless series of incidents of people popping under pressure or getting hit by stray bullets and hurricanes. Then a recovery-movement guru recommends that we just stop watching the news, listing it as one of the five major sources of stress today. And, for a second, there's a pause in the flow as if we stop to wonder if this is the little bit of advice that will finally reach us like a fortune cookie shot straight from the factory to our personal plate to spawn a quiet moment of clear thinking.

Too clear, maybe.

TEENAGERS WHO KILL

We look for a lesson in Columbine and its offshoots; or for a glaring cause like bad parenting (too much parenting? too little parenting? What kind of parenting?); or for some suddenly recognizable copycat phenomenon coming from something in our "society." It's as if some quick knowing of why bad things happen would be a sign that we care, or notice things, if only in retrospect.

But the kids, or the records they leave behind, tell stories that have their own complex trajectories: they're caught in an obsessive focus on the details of a BIG scenario; they're surging to escape a trapped life; they're dangerously depressed; they're alone with their cadre and their plan. These stories don't end in a moral but are left to resonate with all the other ways that intensities rise out of the ordinary and then linger, unresolved, until memory dims or some new eruption catches our attention.

The intensity of erupting events draws attention to the more ordinary disturbances of everyday life. Or it distracts us from them. Or both. It's as if the news of the weird shows what could happen if half-known pressure points, in the wrong hands, were cooked down to some basic craziness and pushed to a violent end. And we're left with the visible signs of relays we can't name or predict and don't know what to do with.

The body hums along, rages up, or deflates. It goes with the flow, meets resistance, gets attacked, or finds itself caught up in something it can't get out of.

It gyrates to mold itself to every new techno-gadget that comes along. The fast, edgy corrections of self-help regimens give it something to do: take an aspirin a day (or not); drink a glass of red wine a day (or not); eat butter, or low-fat margarine, or canola oil; don't eat carbs at all; eat oatmeal to strip the bad cholesterol from your arteries; eat wild Alaskan salmon to add the good cholesterol; try antioxidants or kava kava or melatonin.

Against this tendency, a spate of memoirs works the lone self into a fictional sacrifice powerful enough to drag the world's impacts onto stages. Recovery groups add density to the mix, offering both practical recipes for self-redeeming action and a hard-hitting, lived recognition of the twisted, all-pervasive ways that compulsions permeate freedoms and are reborn in the very surge to get free of them once and for all.[12]

75

GETTING STRAIGHT

Benny has been straight for a year and a half. He starts going to a wild Pentecostal church. Then he decides to start a Bikers for Christ church of his own. The members go to prisons, visiting. Benny has a vision of a big trip to Huntsville or someplace like that. They'll ride in on, like, 150 Harleys and go up the aisles in

[12] See Eve Kosofsky Sedgwick, "Epidemics of the Will," in *Tendencies* (Durham, N.C.: Duke University Press, 1993).

front of all the cages. He can hear the roar of the engines. He sees the bikes and muscled bodies following him in. He feels the eyes of the prisoners on him. He says it'll give them a thrill.

ADDICTION

An old friend, Joyce, calls her with horror stories of trying to save her daughter Lilly from a bad addiction. She says it's like Lilly's in a dream world and she just doesn't care. Joyce realizes how bad things are when she goes to bail Lilly out of jail one night but Lilly refuses to leave her girlfriend and her girlfriend's baby. She demands that her mother go get diapers for the baby as if that's the only thing that matters.

Now Lilly's back staying with Joyce and working at Wendy's. She's saying she wants to get straight so she and her girlfriend and the baby can get a place of their own. Her license has been revoked, so Joyce is spending four hours a day driving her over the mountain to work and picking her up at midnight.

The road is bad, especially at night, and twice this week Joyce has been followed by the same truck and car. The first time they were shooting and she didn't know if they were shooting at her, at each other, or at the road signs. But they finally passed her. The other time they appeared out of the fog right behind her, but after a while they just cut out their lights and disappeared.

One day Joyce called one of the hospitals that advertise addiction programs. They told her it would cost four hundred dollars a day. She said "Are you *crazy?*" She said, "Those ads are wrong that say if you need help you can get it. The rich people can help their kids but not the poor people. Now if I thought I could get off cigarettes I'd stand naked in the four-lane to town. But now wait 'til *you* have kids; you can just kiss your *mind* goodbye."

The closure of "the self" or "community" or some kind of "meaning" is something dreamy that happens in a moment of hope or hindsight. But it's not just ideology or irrelevant fancy, but rather an actual fold or texture in the composition of things.

There are many compositions of subjects and meanings. Some work better than others. Some are smoother, more consistent. Some can be prolonged. Others operate clumsily, break down, and have to be constantly rethought. They can lead to trouble. The difference often depends on what material a person has to work with.

But even those compositions with all the weight of the world behind them are still live. They still get hit by forces that shock and they still make moves to leave themselves behind, even if it's not the smartest thing in the world to do. Or they get stuck and that's not always the smartest thing either. We remain alert to all the possibilities even if we think we know it all.

SCENES OF LIFE

Sometimes the scene of a finished life appears like a beautiful figure on the horizon. For a minute, it's like a snapshot hangs suspended in the air while we watch, wide-eyed. But a little detail out of place can be a telltale sign of something terribly wrong. Or just funny, quirky, a boink in the perfect scene. We're drawn simultaneously to the amazing bubble image and to all the ordinary affects that animate it and pull it apart.

Her mother's painting class has become a support group. She says it really is, because there are interesting people in it, meaning they have interesting lives, meaning they all have their problems—something to talk about and something to hide, too.

Mary is the quiet one who never says a word and everything is always fine with her. But one day she lets something slip about a first husband and they're all over it. To make a long story short, she married the guy who helped her get away from her first husband and now they're so happy they eat low-fat vegetarian food, take all kinds of pills, and measure and weigh everything so they can go on living forever.

Sue's first husband was cheap. He wouldn't spend a dime. He took to his bed on their wedding day and never got up again. He finally committed suicide on the day of her second marriage. The others notice that she talks fast and never seems to sit down.

They suspect Betty comes from money. She's more of the garden club crowd. But her family isn't exactly what you'd call good to her and she lost her only son in a car wreck. She paints too fast; she's just happy to get one thing done and get on to the next one. Her husband makes the little boxes and plaques she needs to keep her busy. She's nice talking but once in a while she'll swear—"That son of a bitch."

Carol's husband quit working because he couldn't take the stress. He roamed around the house all day. Then he decided that most of his stress came from her. He started following her around the house, writing down in a little leather notebook everything she did that stressed him out.

Donna's husband left her and their four kids for a younger woman. She finally found another man but the others are suspicious of him because he told Donna that she was *soooo* beautiful and he said that she was going to turn his life around. (The eyes roll). She has his ring and he's moved in with her and right away he's quit his job and he wants her to sell her house and buy another one because he doesn't want to have to be reminded of her former husband. And it looks like he drinks. She's counting. It looks like it's four cocktails a night, at least.

Her mother, Claire, is the good listener. She doesn't like to air her problems. So the others think she's the one with the perfect life. When she gave them all a copy of Nicholas Sparks's romantic novel *The Notebook*, they decided that was what Claire and her husband were like. One day when one of them was talking about a woman who did something daring she said, "Well I would never do that, but I bet *Claire* would."

LIVE WIRE

Like a live wire, the subject channels what's going on around it in the process of its own self-composition. Formed by the co-agulation of intensities, surfaces, sensations, perceptions, and ex-pressions, it's a thing composed of encounters and the spaces and events it traverses or inhabits.

Things happen. The self moves to react, often pulling itself someplace it didn't exactly intend to go.

HELLO DEARIE

A cheerful e-mail comes from her friend Andrew in Chicago. When he lived in his tiny little house down the street from her, he would stop by, bringing acorns that had dropped in piles on the streets, or dolls or paintings he had made, or stories of found objects, real or imagined. Now it's e-mails coming in and an occa-sional phone call.

Mike was here for the week, and it's always so fun to have him around, and then he has to go, and I get a little blue. O, well, we had a wonderful week and did all sorts of fun things. Yesterday we drove to Wisconsin, not to get apples, though we intended to do that, but rather, it turns out, to snoop on Kenosha and Racine. In Kenosha, which was as cute as a bug, and just about as small, we saw a sign that said "Estate Sale" . . . oh; you can imagine me salivating at that can't you? An estate sale in Sneekcraggle, Wisconsin?! Let's go!

So we do. It's down a regular street of suburban homes. And then down a road that's narrower and the houses smaller, then down a gravel path to homes that are EASILY half the size of my house in Austin! Really! It's like miniature people live on this street. All sorts of trees and bushes separate the homes and the grass is mowed "up to a certain point" and then it's just weeds. The garage with the sale is about six inches below ground level and is filled with the most charming display of things and more things. And it's all half off. I get a cluster of old rusty knives and forks taped together with the price "$1.48 for ALL (8)," and Mike gets two crimson sateen brocade pillows that looked like they are inspired by the Ali Baba-in-the-Harem look. Inside, I can't pass up the crocheted carnations, which you are supposed to use as pulls for your window shades! So many other wonders that we can't or won't buy but it is a lovely dream. And the sellers! Mike and I are ready to move in just to hang out with them. All of them very Wisconsiny, lots of O's and gee-whizzes. There is a room full of Betty Whites! All trying to help us figure out the half price. She keeps saying "O, gee. This is a hard one! One forty-eight! O gee, what would that be, then? Wow, well let's go on to this one, half of twenty-five, well, let's call it twelve cents, ok?" and on like that. I am totally cuted out because they are all over seventy and are wearing Bulls parkas. The day is like that. No apples, but lots of yellow and butterscotch and red trees. Just calming to drive through.

Then another e-mail comes from Andrew about a trip through Virginia. He and Mike are stopped at a traffic light. A gang of punks parades across the street wearing black clothes, safety pins, day-glow hair, and piercings. Andrew beams at them, following their progress with pleasure until one of the women starts pointing at them, screaming something. Andrew stares at her mouth,

dumfounded. What's that she's saying? "Look at the fucking faggots! Fuck you faggots! Fuck you!"

There's a sad silence in the car.

"But how did they know, Mike?"

"Hellooooo! Two men driving in a car together . . . clearly
enjoying themselves . . . wearing sweaters. . . ."

"Oh."

Encounters can happen anywhere. And not the just sad and scary
ones, either.

One day the woman in front of her at the convenience store
turns and stares at her, grinning, a look of dawning recognition
spreading over her tanned young face. Her eyes are ecstatic.

She smiles back at the young woman. Then, after a long moment of locked gazes, she says, "You think you know me." The
young woman nods ever so slightly and heaves a sigh of pleasure.
"Well I live in the neighborhood. Maybe we met through (so and
so)." The woman barely shrugs and slowly puts a finger up to her
lips as if to say, "Hush (little baby, don't you cry)." She sighs again;
her eyes are gleaming.

She slides her money past the young woman to pay the cashier.
"Ok, then. Bye-bye." As she is pulling out of the parking lot she
sees her come out and get on her bike.

She tells the story at home that night and it's decided that of
course the woman was *on* something—acid or ecstasy or *something.*

Oh. Yea. I guess so.

But the smiling image stays with her for a day or two.

The labor of looking has been retooled and upgraded so we can cut back and forth between the images popping up in the living room and some kind of real world out there.

America's Most Wanted airs photos of bank robbers with and without beards so you can scan the faces at the 7-11 for a match. Mimicking the moves of surveillance technologies, the citizenry now practices self-discipline on the level of a bodily impulse. Of course there are refusals too, and all kinds of ambivalence, hesitations, and sidesteps. Practices gathered under the sign of discipline actually have tendrils spreading out to complex and shifting states of attraction and distraction, pleasure and sadness, belonging and longing. Little half-lived games like scanning the faces at the 7-11 are not just a matter of festering alienation or a mean-spirited will to bend others to the rule of law. There is also the simple seduction of the game of recognition itself. Or the fascination with the moment when something snaps into a frame to become more real, or at least more particular. Excesses of all kinds draw special attention—successes and failure, surges of action, wild trajectories that lead somewhere.

There are socialities of the watching. In the convenience store, there is an aggressively casual, noncommittal noticing—half furtive, half bored. If there's a checkout line, it's loose; people mill around waiting. They buy lottery tickets, cigarettes, junk food, and beer. There are those who buy a single giant can of cheap beer early in the morning. There are those who have a habit of two or more trips to the "rip store" a day. There are those who build a routine of going once a day just to get out of the house; to have the transaction of buying something; to make brief, light talk. There are those who only stop in occasionally for a quart of milk or a newspaper because it's efficient and they're busy holding things together.

Differences of all kinds are noted automatically. There is irritation, sometimes amusement, or a hard-boiled, hard-hearted lack of interest in something someone else is doing. And sometimes there are displays of kindness—brief, flickering, half-made gestures that can be noted as a bright moment in the day, or ignored.

THE UTOPIAN HOTEL

She and the baby get stuck overnight in Atlanta. Outside the airport there are banks of phones and a whole parking lot full of hotel shuttles. It's cold and gray. She starts randomly calling for a room, but then a nice shuttle driver gets them one at the Ameri-Suites. He says it's the best place in town, anyway, and not expensive. It's right down the street.

The place is strangely gracious and homey. The clerks are very calm, and next to the front desk there are freezer and refrigerated cases stocked with ordinary frozen dinners, ice cream, and fruit. The suites are huge and they have full kitchens. A man immediately brings up a crib for the baby and sets it up, complete with sheets and a baby blanket. (This never happens in hotels.)

They go down to the lobby to roam around. An impromptu bar has been set up and people are sitting here and there, eating pizza and talking across tables. She asks for a beer and holds out a five-dollar bill. The bartender says "What's that for? It's free. Help yourself to some pizza." In the morning the same room is full of people gathered around a full complementary breakfast buffet, eating together in sleepy intimacy.

The hotel is owned and staffed by African Americans, and everyone, except for a few stragglers like herself, is a person of color. It's like a scene of unexpected hope. A way of doing things differently. A nerve relaxed. A sense of learning. Because for *once* the white people are not in charge of some kind of sensory alarm system.

POWER IS A THING OF THE SENSES

Power is a thing of the senses. It lives as a capacity, or a yearning, or a festering resentment. It can be sensualized in night rages.

It can begin as a secret kept or as a gesture glimpsed in a hallway.

It can be leaked or harvested for future reference.

It can spread like wildflower seeds randomly tossed on a suburban lawn.

We do things *with* power, and *to* it. There are palpable pleasures and acid stomachs in questioning it, spying on it, digging it up, calling it out, evading it, ingratiating oneself to it, sacrificing oneself on its altar, putting something over on it, or somehow coming to rest outside its whirlpool even for a minute.

AGENT ORANGE

The young woman who lives next door starts to pour a gallon jug of Round-Up around a tree in her front yard so she can plant a decorative lawn cover there. Danny runs over to tell the woman she'll kill the trees and poison everything with that stuff. He says it's really just Agent Orange in an over-the-counter jug. He says he doesn't think the woman's all there. A year or two later, she dies in a car accident. Her husband is screaming and smashing walls in the house. Hordes of men move in with him. They hang out on the front porch, drinking beer and heckling women walking by on the street. They get puppies and then neglect them. So the puppies howl all day in the backyard or escape and run around killing neighborhood cats. The men start to fight with each other. The grass grows to four feet tall and they park a large boat on a trailer in the front yard. One day one of them gets in his truck and starts ramming all the other trucks parked over there. Finally, they're evicted. The landlord calls them hippies.

CLOSE ENCOUNTERS

Down the street there's a Vietnam vet with a temper problem. He's in his forties when he marries the woman who owns the tiny house next to her friend Andrew's place. No one knows where he lived before that.

At first, he and Andrew get along well as men borrowing tools and talking about lawns and fences. But then one day Andrew goes out to get his mail wearing a sarong and the guy stares at him pointedly and sneers, "Nice SKIRT." After that he doesn't want to talk to Andrew at all, or even look at him.

Sometimes when she drives by on her way home she sees the guy out in his front yard yelling at cars. Andrew says he gets enraged if someone drives by too fast or something, and he spews foul language at the top of his lungs for a full ten minutes. Andrew says he's never heard anything like it—not even close.

The guy becomes obsessed with raccoons getting into his attic. He starts talking to Andrew again in order to discuss all the niceties of trapping and killing raccoons. Then one day when Andrew comes home the guy is standing in his yard looking shell-shocked. All he says is "Oh! It's bad! It's bad!" He heard the coons in his attic again, after months of coon-proofing strategies, and he just lost it. He got a shotgun and shot big holes in the living room ceiling. Blood and guts dropped out and fell onto his wife's new white carpet.

Now he's standing in the yard, covered with blood, panicked.

AGENCIES

Agency can be strange, twisted, caught up in things, passive, or exhausted. Not the way we like to think about it. Not usually a simple projection toward a future.

It's what we mean by "having a life" (as in "get a life"). But it's caught up in things. Circuits, bodies, moves, connections. It takes unpredictable and counterintuitive forms. It's lived through a series of dilemmas: that action is always a reaction; that the potential to act always includes the potential to be acted on, or to submit; that the move to gather a self to act is also a move to lose the self; that one choice precludes others; that actions can have unintended and disastrous consequences; and that all agency is frustrated and unstable and attracted to the potential in things.

It's not really about willpower but rather something much more complicated and much more rooted in things.

REDEMPTIVE VIOLENCE

Redemption: The recovery of something pawned or mortgaged. A second chance born of suffering and still resonant with loss.

The dream of redemptive violence has become the ready matter of commonplace dreams. Dramas of a clarifying surge of action saturate ordinary life, macho movies, laws, publics, institutions, and diffuse, existential dilemmas of personhood and power. Mythic heroes sacrifice themselves to rebirth the world. Tight little circles of religion wrap themselves in apocalyptic dreams. The nation-state gets tough on crime on behalf of family values. The death penalty comes to stand for the execution of evil itself, one individual at a time. And everyday life is hot with the constant clash of people butting up against each other followed by the consuming dream of righteous revenge.

To say that a thing like redemptive violence is a myth is not to say that it's like a bad dream you can wake up from or an idea you can talk people out of. It's more like a strand in the netting that holds things together. A conduit for bits and pieces of political beliefs, networks, technologies, affinities, dreamed-of possibilities and events.

It can take many forms. It can be a mean pettiness, a dissolute rage, a habit of self-destruction, an overcharged and swollen will, a body in a state of alarm. It can be a derailed sensibility thrashing around at full throttle. Or something really small. It's road rage, or parents whipped into violent deeds to protect their children, or drug addicts slashing at the American dream as they spiral out of it. There's always something a little "off" in the way it plays itself out. A little sad. It's the teenagers who kill, the pipe dreams popping up all over the place, the smoldering resentments in workplaces and intimate spaces. It's Andrea Yates drowning her children to save them from eternal damnation. Or Thomas Junta—the "hockey dad"—killing his son's coach in a fight on the ice. Or Junta's brother, arrested shortly thereafter for assault and battery with a dangerous weapon when he threw a cell phone at a Best Buy employee who wouldn't let him return it without a receipt.

THE NET

Something huge and impersonal runs through things, but it's also mysteriously intimate and close at hand. At once abstract and concrete, it's both a distant, untouchable order of things and a claustrophobically close presence, like the experience of getting stuck in a customer service information loop every time you try to get to the bottom of things.

It's as if a net has grown around a mutating gelatinous substance.

It's also as if the net is full of holes, so that little pieces or whole blobs of things are always falling out of it and starting up some new thing on their own.

It harbors fantasies and fears.

It spawns trajectories.

It sets up a quick relay between things.

It induces both rage and the softly positive sense of being connected and so somehow safe (or not, but at least "in it together").

There's a promise of losing oneself in the flow of things. But the promise jumps in a quick relay to the sobering threats of big business, global warming, the big-box corporate landscape, the master-planned community, the daily structural violence of inequalities of all kinds, the lost potentials, the lives not lived, the hopes still quietly harbored or suddenly whipped into a frenzy.

Either that, or the promise of losing yourself in the flow becomes a dull, empty drifting that you can't get yourself out of.

CONSPIRACY THEORY

Investigative reports, talk shows, TV series, movies, novels, and textbooks present a diffuse, sometimes panicked, sense of struggle against unknown forces—a deep worry that normality isn't normal anymore, that somebody has done something to the way things used to be, that we have lost something, that we have been changed.

Conspiracy theory follows power's secret moves through the telltale signs inscribed on banal surfaces. It takes the vaguely lived sense that something isn't quite right and then snaps it into a puzzle form, a search for underlying causes. It dreams of a return to a pristine past and the redemption of a human agency born in an act of vengeance against the actual state of things. Extremists emerge on the paranoid edge. A profile of the loner/loser snaps into place: the hypervigilant over-the-edge look in his eye; the bottomless rage against the system; the obsessive compilation of signs of what "they" are up to; the guy free-falling into violent action as a spectacle of some kind of crisis of agency.

But there's more to it than this. There's pleasure in conspiracy theory. An intimate knowledge of secret collusions, clandestine activities, and little collaborative worlds of an "us" tracking what "they" are doing. There are the small, inventive interpretive practices, the indeterminate trajectories of where things might go, the panics, the dream of popping up into the limelight with some kind of final truth or something, the moment of the "Ah ha! *That's* what this is all about!"

Conspiracy theory travels through divergent and conflicting routes, articulating a widely shared sensibility of being controlled by an all-pervasive something. It takes for granted that the powers that be are functionaries of the opposing camp; that the problem is structural, and that social structures are mysterious, motivated, intentional, and often malevolent. It nods to an ordinary that is always already mixed up in all of this, and yet it also beckons to a reversal or a return as if a sudden magical jolt could turn things around or something.

A RAINDROP FALLS IN HOUSTON

She's flying back from Guatemala en route to Austin via Houston. Near the end of the flight the pilot announces that there has been heavy rain in the Houston area. The new air traffic control tower has flooded (there's a flaw in the design), and they have shut down the airport. Her plane is short on fuel, so it's diverted to Austin. By the time they land thirty minutes later, Houston has reopened. But then by the time they refuel Houston has shut down again.

The pilot announces that there is no plan. No one can get off the plane since there is no immigration office in Austin. They wait on the runway for nine hours. They run out of water and toilet paper. One man in a wheelchair has to be taken off the plane.

They fly back to Houston, but they have just missed the last plane back to Austin. They're given vouchers for a discount on a hotel and are assigned to flights in the morning. It's 2 AM when they get checked in at the hotel and set off on foot across an urban expanse of highways to find an all-night diner.

The next morning at 6, the lines stretch hundreds of yards outside the terminal. Inside, three lines snake around the lobby filling every inch of it with bodies pressed together. Sometimes the lines cross or merge but no one knows which one is best, or which one they are supposed to be in, or where the lines are going. She endures along with the rest of the passengers. Occasionally an airline employee dressed in red moves through the crowd, drawing frantic questions. But the employees don't know anything. The monitors are dead. At 10 she makes it to a ticket counter and is told that her 9 o'clock flight has long been canceled. The agent says she can book her on a flight the next afternoon. She says no way. Somehow she gets on standby on a flight that might leave in four hours.

Inside the terminal, the working monitors show all flights as "delayed." Hers doesn't show up at all. She wanders around until she finds a gate with a mob of people trying to get to Austin. Later, she gets on a flight. The next morning the news reports that Houston airport is back to normal, and we try to forget, as if nothing happened. Just move on.

TRACKING NUCLEAR WASTE

There are uncertainties (to say the least) in the links between human action and complex systems. Notions of truth and expertise gain purchase in the gap, but sketchy connections also prolifrate in the very effort to solidify some kind of order.

She's in Las Vegas, following the conflict over whether the Department of Energy (DOE) will build a national nuclear waste repository in the desert north of the city. There are regular hearings. The format is always the same. Experts deployed by the DOE say that science can handle the nuclear waste. But this statement only incites reaction. People call them liars and then offer detailed scenarios of what could happen to nuclear waste trucked cross-country from a hundred sites on back roads where local emergency cleanup crews won't have a clue what to do with a nuclear spill. Or they come up with bright ideas about what else the DOE could do with the stuff, like shoot it to the moon or bury it in the ocean floor.

Sometimes the DOE scientists, put on the spot, end up saying the opposite of what they've been brought there to say. They say geology is not a predictive science; there's no saying what might happen to plutonium buried underground for ten thousand years.

One day at a hearing in a casino, the DOE displays a nuclear waste transportation cask so that people can see it and touch it for themselves. They show charts of the DOE chain of command (it's very systematic-looking). Then they show cartoons that parody irrational public fears. One is of a pickup truck piled fourteen-feet high with barrels of nuclear waste. The truck is stopped at the entrance to a New York City tunnel. Workers with beer bellies hanging over their jeans are standing around in traffic looking at a bridge clearance sign that says "eleven feet." One of the barrels has fallen off the truck and is rolling down the ramp into the tunnel. It's the moment of decision. One of the men is saying, "Go for it!" The DOE says their system is not like this. They have technology to circumvent the human factor. They have quality control systems. At one point the DOE general manager places his hand on the nuclear waste cask for a full minute to show that a body doesn't blow up on contact with nuclear waste (of course the cask he has his hand on is empty). Then he invites the public to the parking lot outside to see the cask that has just made the first dry run across the country in an eighteen-wheeler. They go inside the trailer to touch the cask and listen to the loud hum of its "containment systems." It has a lot of flashing lights.

Then she goes up and talks to the truck driver sitting in the cab. He's wearing a cut-off Harley Davidson T-shirt and he has several earrings in one ear. He wants to talk about his high-level security clearance—a G clearance, which is better even than a C clearance. She asks him about the computer keyboard sitting on the passenger seat. He tells her a story. As he was driving away from the origin point in New Jersey, they told him to log in every fifteen minutes so they'd know where he was at all times. He had never used a computer before, so he responded as if it were a joke: "Yeah sure, I'll call you when I get there." But the keyboard turned out to be easy to use—nothing to it. Except that the first time he logged on, the people reading the satellite that was tracking him sent an urgent message asking if he had been rerouted. When he punched in that this was the route he'd been given, he received an alert that he was on the wrong route, which was accompanied by a second urgent request that he specify if he had been rerouted. So he shut off the computer because if he'd had real nuclear material onboard he certainly wasn't going to listen to these people. Anybody could have gotten control of the satellite—terrorists or nuts. There were terrorists out there who'd love to get their hands on this stuff.

He ended up driving cross-country with no system tracking his location, following the route he'd been given by his dispatcher. For three days he was off the grid and they had no idea where he was. Or at least that was his story. And she was happier ending her own day's story there rather than inside with the DOE's claim to the banality of business as usual.

The ordinary is a moving target. Not first something to make sense of, but a set of sensations that incite.

The possibility that something will snap into sense or drift by untapped.

We struggle to trace it with big stories thrown up like billboards on the side of the road.

We track it through projects and lines of progress, failure, reversal, or flight.

We signal its force through dull routine and trouble, through drifting, running in place, and downtime.

It can be traced in conditions like speedup and the banality of built environments.

Or in the direct commodification of the senses.

Or in the way that the consumer is now the citizen.

Or you can find it in all the drugs, or the prison buildup, or the stress registered in neck muscles, or in the little lifeworlds that spring up like blades of grass around the body's compulsions and dreamy surges.

The ordinary moves in the articulations of who cares / laissez-faire attitudes with the apartheidesque hardenings of the lines of race and class. Or in the harsh responsibilities that the individual is given in the game of becoming a winner or a loser. The only two choices now.

AMERICAN DREAM

The American dream comes into a sharp-edged focus.

There are only winners and losers now.

Dream meets nightmare in the flick of an eye.

Haunted sensibilities track unwanted influences and veiled threats in idioms of addiction, dead ends, and conspiracy, while dreams of transcendence and recluse set afloat reckless hopes of winning or escape.

Anxiety ranges without object. But so does the sense of potential.

We lurch between ups and downs as overwrought dreams flop to earth, only to rise up again, inexplicably revitalized, like the monster in a horror movie or the fool who keeps coming back for more.

Lines of flight are fascinating too: the rocketing fortunes of the rich and famous, the dream of a perfect getaway cottage, or the modest success stories of people getting their lives together again.

Free-floating affects lodge in the surface tensions of low-level stress, loneliness, dread, yearning, a sense of innocence, backed up anger, the ins and outs of love.

FLOATING GAMES

Some sink; others claim they can rise above the flow, walk on water.

Some wear their irony like a badge.

There's pleasure in a clever or funny image, or in being able to see right through things.

Or in holing up to watch your favorite bad TV show, or spinning classes at the gym, or singing along to loud music in the car.

Or the drugs of all kinds.

There's the grim pleasure of a meal at a shelter, or a free bus ride because it's an ozone action day, or a whole box of donuts in the dumpster, or a place to sleep on a church floor because it's freezing tonight. But these, of course, are not the same as a little sensory

vacation to liven up your day. More like forced treading water—
the busy work of constantly repeating the unsupported search for
a starting point.

There's the dream of checking out for good.

Or the dream of getting something for nothing.

SLOT MACHINE

The ordinary is a drifting immersion that watches and waits for
something to pop up.

An experiment. Something worth trying that's hiding in plain
sight.

Carrie is a self-styled witch and gypsy. Four feet ten with jet-
black hair below her waist, she does clerical work at a university,
not quite making ends meet. To get out of paying rent, she runs
a free in-house pet-sitting service for traveling faculty. She moves
from house-sit to house-sit. In the down times she stays with
friends.

She's both reckless and hyperorganized. She runs her business with the precision of a corporate middle manager, but once
she risked everything on a love affair that took her to Australia
and stranded her there when things went badly. In Australia, she
learned she had a talent for gambling. She made enough money
playing cards to buy her ticket home and have a few thousand
dollars left over to get situated back in the states.

Now she takes quick trips to Nevada, stopping at the first cheap
casino on the border. There are always stories . . . She walks into
the casino and immediately spots a machine with an aura. But
the time isn't right, so she waits it out. She checks in, watches
part of a James Bond movie on TV in her room, and then goes
back to check the machine. The time is almost right. She chats
with the woman at the next machine, listens to the band in the
bar, drifts by the machine again, watches another TV show, and

finally returns to the machine. It's after midnight. She sits down at the machine and concentrates. The woman at the next machine (who is still there) stands behind her to cheer her on. She plays a couple of dollar slots and hits the jackpot. She gives the neighbor a cut because she figures her cheering helped and it's good karma anyway. Later that night, she returns to the same machine and it pays off again.

Carrie says it's hard to explain how she knows when a machine is right; it's just a feeling. Some machines are just for fun, some are serious, but they all hold some promise of a payoff. Her talent for spotting the promise in a machine lends substance to the dream of beating the odds, and it turns the vague but compelling hope of "coming out a winner" into the sensory practice of keeping her eyes on the prize through the din and the flashing lights. Her gambling is not just the residue or symptom of distantly determining forces but an actual instance of affective and material emergence—a singularity that literally catches her attention and holds it long enough for her to do something with it.

PUSHING IT

One day, when she's living in a trailer park in Las Vegas, she meets a young man in the community hot tub. He's just moved from the Midwest. He can stay here with family for a little while, but he's already found a job humping tires for minimum wage. He shows her a missing finger lost at work the first week on the job. He talks about it as if it were like losing a fingernail or something. Something to be expected from a young man's work.

This reminds her of stories about people who injure themselves for cash. Stories that turn a routine desperation into an odd moment fueled by a character. Stories that add a weird form of agency or life (or something) to the hard core of desperation, adding up to something like desperation plus.

There's the story, for instance, of the old miner in West Virginia who thwacked off his own fingers for workman's compensation every time he was sick or needed money until he only had one finger left and couldn't work at all anymore. Or there's the "lake snake" outside Austin who collected insurance money by claiming he slipped on a banana in the supermarket. Later, he accidentally shot himself in the leg, becoming completely disabled. He was drinking hard. There's a story genre in cowboy poetry about a cowboy who injures himself in an accident out on the range. He loses a toe or cuts an artery in his leg. There's lots of blood, but he just puts on his boot and drives himself a long distance into town. By the time he gets to the hospital he's barely conscious and the blood is pouring out of the top of his boot.

These stories take the trajectory of expected or accepted injury at work to an end point outside ordinary rationales. They run away with things. In them, anything's possible and weird forms of agency and tricky moves become real in twisted bodies. Body parts become actual commodities that can be converted into modest cash payments in a pinch.

They say Lawrence, Massachusetts, is the insurance fraud capital of the state. An insurance fraud was uncovered when a grandmother who was sitting in the back seat of a car was killed in a deliberate head-on high-speed crash with another car. Both drivers were charged with fraud. Runners would find the drivers and then steer them to the lawyers and doctors who would fill out the personal injury reports for a cut.

The effort to get by can quickly become a self-defeating accident, especially when people are pushing it (but not only then).

FREE FALLING

There are bodies out of place.

There are plenty of people in free fall.

There are people whose American dreaming is literally a dreaming cut off from any actual potential. But that doesn't stop it—far from it.

This situation isn't exactly functional but it's not necessarily "bad" either. Though it can be.

PIPE DREAMS

She remembers a night in West Virginia. A group of striking miners sits waiting to see the doctor in the poor people's health clinic. Their bodies are huddled together, their eyes are focused on the dark looming hills outside, they talk in a slow, intimate rhythm of story and ruminative pause. It's the end of a long contract strike and it's suddenly clear that the strike will fail spectacularly. Everyone is saying that the union is dead, that the mines are closing down for good this time, that the miners have been reduced to "company sucks." You can feel the mantra of stunned defeat settle on the room. Heavy talk gives way to even weightier pauses filled only with the shallow, suffocating breathing of men with black lung disease.

Then Johnny Cadle starts in on an elaborate fantasy. Someday they will scale the big brick walls of Governor Rockefeller's mansion and loot it for all it's worth. The others draw their focus to the story. Power grows palpable in the image of high brick walls that can be breached by a potent, collective, working-class masculinity, and then broken up, as if tactile, and dispersed like loot.

The story lurches up and passes in an odd moment. It works not as a representation of a real possibility or a model for action, but instead as a live event—a fleeting conduit between the lived and the potential hidden in it (or hidden from it). Potentiality resonates in its scene. It's an experiment compelled by the drag of affect in the room, and when it's over the men just sit calmly together, as if something has happened.

She hears a story of a botched robbery. Two young street guys, barely twenty, have been on their own now for some time. They try to get work but they have no car, no ID. They try to get a driver's license or food stamps, but their borrowed car breaks down, their twelve dollars gets stolen, and they can't stand to sit all day at the food stamp office getting jerked around. They brag that one day they'll go out in a blaze. They'll rob a bank or something and shoot the rich people. The older guys on the street are always talking about making their big exit in a violent flash, especially if they ever found out they had cancer or the end of the world was coming or something. They say they'd do it, they really would, and it's as if a flash of agency would catapult them off the streets and into the limelight. Or at least it would provide some kind of real ending to a life. Or something.

But these two young guys actually tried to bring their little easy-desperate plan to life. One day they just walked up the road and tried to rob a convenience store with a baseball bat. The police caught them before they got five blocks away. They went to jail— no money, no parole. They got twenty-five years. The others shake their heads. That's *stupid*. This is Texas.

99

DREAM CUTS

She clips a notice from the *New York Times*:

Life Sentence Is Imposed in 3 Kidnapping Killings
WHEATON, ILL.—A jury on Monday sentenced a man to life in prison for killing his pregnant exgirlfriend and two of her children,

and kidnapping his nearly full-term son from her womb. The man, Lavern Ward, 26, denied taking part in the killings. Mr. Ward had been found guilty of the 1995 slayings of Debra Evans, 26, and her daughter, Samantha, 10, and her son, Joshua, 7. He was also convicted of kidnapping the baby, who survived and is being cared for by Ms. Evans's father.

The story takes her back to a visit with friends in the country. Five women in a kitchen are trying to piece together the details of the murders. A man and his new girlfriend cut the baby right out of his ex-girlfriend's belly! What in the world! Then the new girlfriend took the baby home like it was her own, like no one would notice! The women are puzzling this over. Maybe she just wanted a baby, or not a baby, exactly, but the little fame of instant motherhood.

She thinks it must have been like a weirdly literal surge to have a picture-perfect life. It's as if, in the act of turning image into matter, things got out of hand.

The women imagine it must have been like being in a dream you can't wake up from, but it's not real.

Then the weird murder story prompts the memory of another story about the guy down the road who stole from his father so his father sent him to the pen. When he got out, he killed his father and chopped him up in twenty-some pieces. He raped his stepmother and took her and the car. She got away from him and called the police.

The women talk about drugs and demons. They say nothing in *this* world would make any of *them* do a thing like *that*.

Later, there's another story in the paper about a toddler kidnapped from a greyhound bus station in Chicago on Christmas Eve. The kidnapper had told her boyfriend in prison that she had had his baby. So when he was getting out she had to make good on her claim. She hung out at the bus station. She struck up a conversation with a young woman traveling with two small children.

She offered to give them a ride home to Milwaukee. She offered to wait with the younger daughter while the woman went to cash in their bus tickets. Then she took off running with the little girl. They soon found her at home with the little girl in another state. As it turned out, this was not the first time she had been arrested for child abduction.

These are not the only stories of people lurching toward a dream. Stories like this pop up all over the place.

WAL-MART

Stories are leaking out about Wal-Mart locking in workers at night to prevent employee theft. Michael Rodriquez was stocking shelves on the overnight shift at the Sam's Club in Corpus Christi when an electronic cart driven by another employee smashed his ankle. There was no manager with a key to let him out, and the workers had been told they would be fired if they used the fire exit for any reason other than a fire. It took an hour for a manager to get there while Mr. Rodriquez hopped around yelling, "like a hurt dog in the street."

In other lock-ins, a worker in Indiana suffered a heart attack; a stocker in Savannah, Georgia, collapsed and died when paramedics couldn't get in; a hurricane in Florida nearly destroyed a store; and women have gone into labor in stores all over the country. Some workers recall management telling them that the fire doors could not physically be opened, but they would open, like magic, if the fire alarm were triggered. Some recall fire doors that were chained shut.

Wal-Mart officials say they are a very large company with over thirty-five hundred stores. They say locking people in is certainly not something Wal-Mart condones. It's not policy, they can tell us that much.

Wal-Mart prohibits paid overtime work. So night-shift employees clock out at the fortieth hour on the fifth night of the week, usually around 1 AM. Then they sit around napping, playing cards, or watching television until a manager arrives at 6 AM to let them out.

WHIRL-MART

Whirl-Marters are the culture jammers of shopping. Like hoaxing, hacking, and billboard banditry, whirl-marting is an immanent critique that immerses itself in media machines and built environments to leave some kind of mark that gives pause, or to stick to a slippery surface where critiques launched from a full-blown order of right and wrong, true and false, might just slide off.

Whirl-Marters go on nonshopping sprees. They push empty carts around the store in a procession, wearing identical Whirl-Mart T-shirts. Surveillance cameras in the ceiling watch their strange progress through the store. But Whirl-Marters make their own videos of getting thrown out or of store managers screaming at them: "If you're gonna spend so much time in here, pick up an application!!" "The customers *like* our store!" "Number one, man, on the fortune five hundred. WE'RE NUMBER ONE!"

Once some Whirl-Marters alerted the media that they were going to bring a live chicken into a store to barter for an item of clothing made in a third world sweatshop. Police and managers formed a human wall to block the chicken's entrance. So the Whirlers got in their cars and drove around the parking lot playing an antiWal-Mart polka cranked up high on their stereos. Then they put the whole scene up on the Web.

Seven prisoners escape from a south Texas prison. The police find the escape truck in a nearby Wal-Mart parking lot, where the surveillance cameras have captured the escapees on film. The prisoners then rob a Radio Shack, and they check into an Econo Lodge under assumed names. On Christmas Eve they rob an Oshman's sporting goods store, steal a cache of weapons, and kill a local police officer. They remain at large for a month. A reward is offered. Stories circulate. They're like outlaws in the movies on the run from the law. Or like the banditos of Tex-Mex corrido fame who evaded the Texas Rangers on horseback and were spotted all over the state. At one point there are snowstorms in Arkansas and Oklahoma, but people can't buy chains for their tires because the Texas state police came through and bought them all.

Some say the Texas 7 are nice guys. They didn't kill any of the prison guards during their escape. They're friends, human beings. They love their wives. The police say they're hardened criminals and cop killers. Prosecutors ask for the death penalty before they're even caught. So then there's talk of the death penalty and the effects of the prison buildup, the unbelievable overcrowding in the prisons.

The owner of an RV park in Colorado watches *America's Most Wanted* and thinks he recognizes the Texas 7 as the men living in one of his trailers. But he isn't sure. At first, he doesn't turn them in. He's not sure it's his place to do so anyway. He talks it over with his wife.

Meanwhile, one of the men joins a local church and starts leaving the trailer to go to services. People see him several times at church. He's the one they can definitely identify. The owner of the park decides to turn them in.

They stayed together (a mistake) because they were friends and because they had to get IDs and jobs before they could split up.

When the police arrive, they find three of the men in a Jeep Cherokee parked outside the trailer. Two more men are inside; one surrenders peacefully but the other commits suicide with a pistol. They discover the last two a couple of days later, hiding out in a nearby Holiday Inn. Before they're arrested, they make some live radio broadcasts denouncing the state's justice system, adding at the end that "the system is as corrupt as we are."

Details continue to circulate about the lives of these men, especially the "ringleader," George Rivas. He's very intelligent. Born in El Paso, raised by his grandparents after the divorce of his parents, he dreamed of being a police officer. But he didn't participate in high school activities. He named his dogs Ruger and Baretta, after guns. A year after graduating from high school he committed his first robbery and burglary, for which he was sentenced to ten years of probation. He enrolled as a general studies major at the University of Texas at El Paso, but two years later he started a string of robberies: a Radio Shack, an Oshman's sporting goods store, a Toys 'R Us. In prison he made trustee status and worked in the prison's maintenance department, one of the best duty assignments. He became disillusioned (he had been sentenced to life in prison). He spent his nights confined to an austere eight-by-eight foot cell equipped with only a bunk, a wash basin, and a toilet . . . he was sick of the lousy food . . . he was tired of hearing the metal doors slide shut when he returned to his cell at lockdown.

When he's captured, his own words are about justice and rage. He's very articulate.

PUBLIC SPECTERS

Public and private spheres are drawn into a tight circuit, giving the ordinary the fantasy quality of a private life writ large on the world. Publicly circulating styles, sensibilities, and affects simultaneously snap into place in hearts all over the country.

Public specters have grown intimate. There are all the bodies lined up on the talk shows, outing their loved ones for this or that monstrous act. Or the reality TV shows where the camera busts in on intimate dramas of whole families addicted to sniffing paint right out of the can. We zoom in to linger, almost lovingly, on the gallon-sized lids of paint cans scattered around on the living room carpet. Then the camera pans out to focus on the faces of the parents, and even the little kids, with rings of white paint encircling cheeks and chins like some kind of self-inflicted stigmata.

Trauma TV morphs into split, schizophrenic trajectories. Vicious spectacles of pain and dysfunction are followed by the thirty-second therapeutic sound-bite. We dive back into an intense encounter with *something*, no matter how fabricated. Then we reach the saturation point and stop watching.

One day there is an old man in a wheelchair on an afternoon talk show. The tears run down his face as he tells the story of a day in 1976. His old lady has left him and he's raising his two-year-old daughter alone. When he gets up to go to the bathroom, his daughter, who is playing on the porch, goes over and drinks from a can of kerosene that a neighbor had left for him that morning. His story launches into graphic details: he has a broken-down car in the driveway, with no plates on it, and his driver's license has been revoked for drunk driving. But it's an emergency so he just puts the baby in the car and takes off flying. When he gets to town, the traffic's backed up and people won't let him through the red light. He's screaming: "I've got a *baby* in here and she's drunk *kerosene*! I've got to get her to the *hospital*!" He runs the red light and someone hits him hard and breaks his neck. When the police get there, they take the baby to the hospital because he's still managing to scream about the kerosene, but they don't let him go with her. They take him off to jail for driving without a license. When they get the little girl to the hospital, they see that she has scrapes on her knees from playing on the cement porch, and they decide to take her away from him. The last time he sees her is on July 6th in the welfare office by the elevators. She's crying frantically. He tells her, "Don't cry, poodle doggie, daddy's gonna come back and get you some day." And that's the last day he sees her. He's been looking for her ever since.

On the talk show, father and daughter are reunited. They hug and kiss. Then he looks at his daughter, his mouth trembling and the tears pouring down his face, and says, "I *wanted* you, poodle dog, I wanted to *keep* you, I *always* wanted *you*, honey!"

The nightmarish realities on display in the scene of public viewing are unthinkable, ridiculous, and ritually replayed with only slight variations. It's not like the scenes are supposed to be ideals or warning signs. They capture a haunted potential. Things go off on trajectories. They're pushing something. "Pushing the envelope" is a light, popular phrase but it might not capture the state of things.

THE ORDINARY CAN TURN ON YOU

The ordinary can turn on you.

Lodged in habits, conceits, and the loving and deadly contacts of everyday sociality, it can catch you up in something bad. Or good.

Or it can start out as one thing and then flip into something else altogether.

One thing leads to another. An expectation is dashed or fulfilled. An ordinary floating state of things goes sour or takes off into something amazing and good. Either way, things turn out to be not what you thought they were.

One day Sissy's husband, Bud, came home talking about a real smart guy who told him that the economy is going bust. Something about how the price of gold would go way up and they'd have to print up a whole different kind of money—red money. Bud thinks that means that the color of the money will be red, but Sissy thinks the guy's talking about communist money somehow. "But who cares? My money isn't worth anything anyway," she says. They say the value of gold is all imaginary—and diamonds too. People say they're the best investment, but she just saw an episode of *60 Minutes* on how the diamond mines are controlled by a cartel and jewelers can't tell the difference between zirconium and diamonds, anyway. "Just my luck," she thinks. "I always thought I could bank on my wedding rings."

IDENTITY SURGES

Racism can be a live texture in the composition of a subject. So can dreams of racial utopia.

People of color often smile at her and her daughter in the supermarket. They strike up conversations. They say the baby is so cute. A tension seems to release, as if a white woman with a brown baby provides an opening for public encounter.

Other times, they get vicious stares from white people in restaurants or at swimming pools. You can't tell by looking at people who it will be. Sometimes it's young, hip-looking women who do it. It's a demanding, persistent stare that says, "What do you think you're doing?" or "Who do you think you are, parading around in public like this." It amazes her. She get tense, enraged. She stares them down. "Who are these people?" "Who do they think they are?"

She wonders what they've been reading and what church they go to or what it is, exactly, that animates them and this trouble.

SUBURBAN APOCALYPTICISM

The Calvary Chapel church emerged during the Jesus movement of the 1970s. It drew converts through Christian rock festivals, go-go clubs, love-ins, coffeehouses, surfer clubs, baptisms in the ocean, and hotlines for kids on bad trips, including a thirty-second cure for heroine addiction. Now it's morphed into a huge network of suburban evangelical megachurches that mix hyperconservative apocalypticism with a hip style—or, rather, a multicultural mall style.

The church hosts weekly meetings of the Working Women's Joyful Life Bible Study, Proverbs Class for Men, High School Mothers' Prayer Meeting, New Spirit Alcohol and Drug Recovery, Singles' Group, Prison Fellowship, and the Physically Disabled Fellowship. Its bookstores offer books on the end-times symptoms of liberal humanism and Christian self-help books. The world is in a steady moral decline. Kids who spend all their time on computer games no longer play kick-the-can and hide-and-seek. The storytellers are no longer the parents and teachers; instead, the huge media conglomerates have taken on the role. But the pastor offers practical tips on how to be a Christian in the end times: try talking to non-Christians at holiday parties, do lunch with a co-worker or invite neighbors for dinner, invite non-Christian men to watch the game with you, make contacts when you're working out or at kids' events, contact people you used to know ("Though *some*, it's better *not* to look 'em up, know what I'm *sayin'*?").

Wednesday is movie night at the church. Christian horror movies show scenes of teenagers who miss the plane to the rapture because they are too distracted by a Walkman to hear the final boarding call. Businessmen miss the flight because they're on their cell phones and portable computers doing business or playing video games.

Thursday night is the Christian Prophecy Update Meeting, which is attended, it seems, by the church's extremists. Evil forces are evident in federal gun control, unisex bibles, environmentalism, sex education in the schools, and the spread of homosexuality through the media. False knowledge systems have produced ludicrous claims posing as mainstream values and common sense. Christians have to learn to read between the lines. A man's computer might suggest that he call his wife his "spouse," and the story of Peter and the Wolf is suddenly about an endangered species. A person with measles can be quarantined, while a person with AIDS cannot even be legally identified. Gun-control nuts want to ban toys that even resemble guns. It's a crime to have a shouting match with your wife. The war on drugs is just an excuse to control us. The IRS suddenly has the right to access our bank accounts. They're building up the backbone of the Internet with new fiber and the government can't control it. But don't bother to pay your taxes because the Lord is coming soon.

BODY FOR LIFE

Anyone can find herself caught up in a little world. Sooner or later, everyone does. Something comes into view and you find yourself participating in the apparatus that made it.

She takes up *Body for Life* on the advice of a friend. Between them, it's a joke. They call it their cult. But they also know there's something *to* a little extreme self-transformation, or at least the effort.

Body for Life is a best-selling bodybuilder's book with glossy before-and-after pictures on the covers. "Twelve weeks to mental and physical strength." It's a challenge to put down the beer and chips and start loving life, not just living it; thriving, not just surviving.

She isn't at all taken with the oiled, muscle-man and muscle-woman pictures, but the little game of moving back and forth between the before-and-after shots literally catches her eye. The eye jumps from the fat and pale to the tanned and muscled. Peek-a-boo. All the bodies are white. They remind her of the body displays she was always running into in Las Vegas at the post office, or at the drive-in movie theater, or while waiting in line to get a new driver's license. The half-naked bodybuilders with wet-skinned snakes draped around their necks, or a monkey on a leash, or a stars-and-stripes halter top and permed blonde hair.

Her friend calls the people in the pictures "beef cakes." Class seems to be somehow involved in all this (but if you ask anyone they swear up and down that the people into *Body for Life* come from all walks of life). A "mainstream" emerges out of it as the will to change and the game of imagining the fruits of success. In this mainstream—a space of promise—it's as if people can be catapulted out of the back seat of life and flighty, self-defeating dreams can be made vital, generative flesh. There are testimonies of the breakthroughs that happened when people were looking at the pictures, or watching the inspirational video you get for a fifteen-dollar donation to the Make-A-Wish Foundation. Suddenly released from sluggish banality and the feeling of being all alone, people begin to crave the twelve-week program even more than they crave ice cream, chocolate, chips, and beer.

There's nothing weird about how this happens. It's laid out like a twelve-step program in which spiritual transformation flows directly through the flesh. First you ask yourself hard questions and write down the answers. You create twelve weekly goals and voice them with mimicked confidence every morning and night until the confidence is real. You create five daily habits. You commit. You focus. You surrender the negative emotions that hold everyone back; you start looking forward. Everyone who takes up the twelve-week challenge is a winner. You imagine other people gazing approvingly at your new body until that image becomes you. You realize you will never again get sidetracked.

She isn't interested in the inspirational business and she never actually reads the book. She plays the game of the before-and-after photos and then goes directly to the food and exercise charts at the end of the book. She gets organized. She makes copies of the charts so she can fill them out every day like a diary. She memorizes the acceptable foods and stocks up. She ritualizes each meal and gleefully eats whatever she wants on the seventh day of the week, as instructed. She orders boxes of the shakes and power bars. She experiments with the recipes that make the chocolate shake taste like a banana split and the vanilla shake taste like key lime pie. She gets the picture. She feels the surge. She lets it become a piece of her. Then there are the inevitable ups and downs, the sliding in and out of *Body for Life*'s partial cocoon. Over time, she reduces the program to a few new prejudices about how to exercise and what to eat.

Later, she stumbles on Body for Life Community.com — a network of dozens of chat rooms. Some are Christian fellowships that make *Body for Life* their gospel: "Carry the message or wither . . . those who haven't been given the truth may not know the abundant life we have found — a way out, into life, a real life with freedom." Others are organized by area and look exactly like personal ads with pictures.

In the chat rooms, things get really concrete. One woman confesses that she can smell the chocolate right through the wrappers in the bowl of Halloween candy by the door, and someone shouts support in capital letters: HANG IN THERE! YOU CAN DO IT!!! A man happily obsesses about how to prepare his shakes. "My favorite is chocolate and to prepare the shake I always use 3 cubes of ice from the Rubbermaid mold, put them (without water) in the jar and then pour the water in. Use twelve and a half ounces and 1 centimeter, then blend for about fifty-five seconds. You got to use a stopwatch! I think this is why I love Myoplex, because I blend it for more seconds and I drink it cool without milk or bananas."

Connections between people are important: "Good morning to everyone. Been off for a few days. Lizzy—sorry to hear about your migraine—scary! Jim—it's true—your pictures don't do you justice! Abs—I love your philosophy! It's true—we become what we think about. Deb—Congratulations! Good luck with your photos—can't wait to see your progress! If you find something that covers bruises, let me know—I bruise just thinking about bumping into something. Can't wait to see you all at the upcoming events!"

There are support groups for the dieting and for ongoing troubles and tragedies.

The public face of *Body for Life* is made of excessive self-expressions that proclaim, confess, obsess, and gush. Not because the body really does just get on track and stay there, but because it slumps and gets sidetracked and rejoins its *Body for Life* self. It wants and it doesn't want; it might do one thing or another. It noses its way along the track its on until it comes across a something. The half-formed trajectories are always the most compelling. It's when the body is in a partly unactualized state and unanchored that it feels most intimate, familiar, and alive. When the body is beside itself, it pulses in the mutual impact of dream and matter, hesitation and forward thrust. It wants to be part of the flow. It wants to be in touch. It wants to be touched. It flexes its muscles in a state of readiness, hums like a secret battery kept charged, registers stress in a back spasm or a weak limb.

Body for Life says turning fleeting fantasies into a vital force is about making a decision, but making a decision is itself about playing games, looking at pictures, following recipes, mimicking desired states, inventing social imaginaries, and talking to yourself in the mirror. The proliferating cultures of the body spin around the palpable promise that fears and pleasures and forays into the world can be made productive, all-consuming passions. But getting on track is not the simple, sober choice of a lifetime but rather a tightrope from which you can topple into ordinary sloppiness or an "epidemic of the will" like obsessive dieting.[13] And after any decision, the body returns to its ordinary buzz.

THE BODY SURGES

The body surges. Out of necessity, or for the love of movement.

Lifestyles and industries pulse around it, groping for what to make of the way it throws itself at objects of round perfection.

The way it builds its substance out of layers of sensory impact.

The way the body is submerged in a flow and both buoyed and carried away. It strains against recalcitrant or alien forces, or it drifts downstream, eyes trained on the watery clouds overhead.

Agency lodged in the body is literal, immanent, and experimental. It no sooner starts out than it gets sidetracked or hits a wall and then holes up, bulks up, wraps itself up. It might pull itself together or pull a veil around itself, build a nest of worn clothing redolent with smells of sweat, or cheap perfume, or smoky wood fires burrowed into wool. If it gets sluggish, it might call for sweet and heavy things to match its inner weight, or for salt and caffeine to jolt it to attention.

The body knows itself as states of vitality, immersion, isolation, exhaustion, and renewal.

It can be alert to the smell of something sweet or rancid in the air or to a movement too quick, a gesture that's a little off.

It can be ponderous, too, gazing on its own form with a zenlike emptiness. As a new lover, it dotes on revealed scars and zones in

113

[13] Sedgwick, "Epidemics of the Will," 130–42.

on freckles and moles and earlobes. As one of the anxious aging, it's drawn to the sight of new jowls and mutant hairs and mottled skin in the bathroom mirror.

The body is both the persistent site of self-recognition and the thing that always betrays us. It dreams of redemption but it knows better than that too.

It loves and dreads the encounters that make it. It latches onto a borrowed intimacy or a plan of some sort.

Layers of invented life form around the body's dreamy surges like tendons or fat.

THE OWL

She's at a Laurie Anderson show at the Soho Guggenheim. The show is called "Your Fortune, $1." A white plastic owl is perched on a stool in a darkened corner spewing out a stream of two-bit advice, trenchant commentary, and stray advertising lingo. Its mechanical yet sensuously grainy voice drones on and on, transfixing her in a flood of Hallmark greeting card schlock. But somehow the owl's simple repetitions intensify the ordinary background noise of slogans and cries of alarm, giving it a sensory texture that is at once deadening and weirdly ponderous.

Then the owl says something she swears she was just unconsciously chanting to herself: "Sometimes when you hear someone scream it goes in one ear and out the other. Sometimes it passes right into the middle of your brain and gets stuck there."

SOMETIMES WHEN YOU HEAR SOMEONE SCREAM . . .

A train wails in the still of the night. It often wakes her. Or it lodges in her sleep, reemerging as a tactile anxiety in the dawn.

She scans her dreamy brain for what might have happened or what might be coming. The morning air is saturated with the smells of kumquat trees and mimosa blossoms and the sounds of mourning doves and pet parrots that long ago escaped their cages and now breed in the trees.

She knows why the train cries. Danny's friend Bobby passed out on the tracks one night and was killed. He and his old lady had been down at the free concert on the river. This is a charged event for the street people. There are graceful moments: a dance gesture, a wide-open smile, a sudden upsurge of generosity, the startled amplitude of pariahs suddenly rubbing shoulders with the housed on a public stage, perhaps even playing the role of party host, making announcements or giving directions or advice. There are crashes too: the people falling down drunk in front of the stage, the vomiting, a man huddled and pale, too sick to party tonight. There are fights.

That night Bobby had a fight with his old lady and stomped off alone. He followed the train tracks to the camp. Then, in Danny's story, Bobby sat alone on the tracks, taking stock in a booze-soaked moment of reprieve. Bobby loved the romance of the train: the high, lonesome sound in the distance, the childhood memory of the penny laid on the tracks, the promise of movement, the sheer power. He lay down and closed his eyes. Then, in the middle of the long train passing, he raised his head, awakening. They say if he hadn't, the train would have passed right over him. But who can sleep with a train passing by overhead?

Sometimes now she gets stuck at the railroad crossing waiting for the train to pass. One day, a boxcar full of Mexican immigrants drifted slowly by, waving and smiling as if they were staging their own welcome to the United States. Another time she drifted into a memory of the coal mining camps in West Virginia where the coal trains would block for hours the only road in and out of town. People would get out and lean on their trucks to talk.

Once a quiet claim began to circulate that someday somebody was going get a pile of dynamite, blow the train in half, and clear the road for good.

The train shapes a story of abjection mixed with vital hopes. Something in the exuberant waving of the new immigrants, the explosive claims in the coal camps, or Bobby's lying down to sleep on the tracks, suggests an intoxicated confidence that surges between life and dream. It's as if the train sparks weighted promises and threats and incites a reckless daydream of being included in a world.

This is the daydream of a subject whose only antidote to structural disenfranchisement is a literal surge of vitality and mobility. A subject whose extreme vulnerability is rooted in the sad affect of being out of place, out of luck, or caught between a rock and a hard place, and who makes a passionate move to connect to a life when mainstream strategies like self-discipline or the gathering of resources like a fortress around the frail body are not an option. A subject who is literally touched by a force and tries to take it on, to let it puncture and possess one, to make oneself its object, if only in passing. A subject for whom an unattainable hope can become the tunnel vision one needs to believe in a world that could include one.[14]

This kind of thing happens all the time. It's an experiment that starts with sheer intensity and then tries to find routes into a "we" that is not yet there but maybe could be. It's a facility with imagining the potential in things that comes to people not despite the fact that it's unlikely anything good will come of it but rather because of that fact.

It's as if the subject of extreme vulnerability turns a dream of possible lives into ordinary affects so real they become paths one can actually travel on.

[14] See Rajchman, *The Deleuze Connections*, 140–44, for a discussion of how all "belief in the world" is lodged in sensation.

Abject and unlivable bodies don't just become "other" and unthinkable. They go on living, animated by possibilities at work in the necessary or the serendipitous.

THE VITAL, SWEET, AND SAD

Some who live on the edge claim a certain craziness; for others it's very much nose to the grindstone, running in place to keep the wolves at bay.

The wild ones say they're wide open and they spend their lives suffering the consequences. It's like they never learn; it's like they use themselves as testing grounds for the forces at play in the world.

They build their identities out of impacts and escapes. They push things to see where they'll go.

Danny grew up in a place in rural North Carolina where young men earned the honorific title of being called by their full names—"Danny Webb"—by doing crazy things that took nerve and skill and a complete disregard for what could happen to them. Like the time Danny climbed, drunk, to the top of a telephone pole in a lightning storm, balanced precariously on the top, arms thrown open, and then fell. Or the time he was in a hurry to get to the beer store before it closed, so instead of taking the road, he drove straight through a mile of tobacco fields, tearing up a path through the crops. Then he used the path whenever he needed to, even after the owner of the fields tried to shoot him.

Danny has stories. Stories filled with mad, momentary victories and violent impacts suffered. And stories filled with wild surges to somehow radicalize the world through sacrifice.

One Christmas, when he and some friends had been drinking heavily all day, they decided to attack the life-sized wooden Santa Claus propped up in the living room. After a few rounds, Danny grabbed a meat cleaver and ran across the room, plunging the knife deep into the wood. His hand slid down the blade, leaving two fingers cut to the bone and one hanging off. But the high point of his story is the scene of getting pulled over by a cop while he and his friends were speeding down the highway to the hospital in an old pickup in the middle of the night. Still drunk, they told the cop it was an emergency and he told them to get out of the truck. Danny said, "No, really," and opened the towel pressed around his wound. The blood gushed out, spurting all over the windows to the rhythm of his heartbeat. Some of the blood hit the cop's face. His face went white and he waved them on, shouting, "Go! Go!"

Danny and his friends have big parties out in the country or at "the compound," where he has finally settled down in a hard and sweet utopia/hell down by the tracks. They play music all night and the music resonates in their bodies: Matt becomes fiddle, Danny becomes guitar, Rebecca becomes mandolin. They build a bonfire, smoke some ribs, tell stories.

Sometimes they perform an attack on the American dream, like smashing a television set and throwing the pieces on the bonfire while they dance around it.

They cherish derelict spaces. They occupy a zone of indeterminacy. They're slippery.

They live the life of a sheer collaboration produced through circuits of debts, gifts, affects, and hard necessities. If one of them finds work, he will cut the others in. When they work, they work hard and fast. They build fences and furniture and sheds, cut down massive trees, xeriscape flowerbeds, haul brush, run electricity or plumbing. They gear up for a big job and then knock it out. Then they party while they're still sweaty, exhausted, satisfied, together.

In the down times, there are long days of hanging out in living rooms set up in the fields beside their shacks. Days of peace or helpless despair. There are art projects built out of rusted metal and aged wood. There are love affairs. There are rages, fights, addictions, hunger, sickness, withdrawal, suicide. There are those who come unhinged at times. Those who float, unable to connect desire to reality. There are days, or weeks, or months, or years, of sad, exhausted, emptiness. There is crazy talk about shooting conservative presidents and robbing banks, taking a few rich people with you on your way out.

They are living the rhythm of a struggle to wrest a "something" out of an everyday life saturated with dragging, isolating intensities of all kinds. More often than not, this is not really a willful act but more like an undoing or a willing mutation that draws the subject into the prepersonal zone of affect.

One thanksgiving, Danny spent hours handing out flowers to people on a busy street. It was like he was trying to jump start a zone of contact in the world.

Another time, he tried to get a commercial coffee pot installed at the VA hospital for the guys in long-term rehab, so they could have their own pot and a place to gather. He called businesses until he found a Mr. Garcia who was very happy to help. Mr. Garcia donated a huge, used, stainless steel, commercial coffeemaker with three burners. Danny borrowed a truck, picked up the coffeemaker, drove it the ninety miles to the hospital and installed it. There was a lot of paperwork. He called a couple of weeks later to see if it was working out. A clerk said they weren't letting patients use it because it was a used machine. He said well, if the patients couldn't use it he was going to come pick it up. Then he started making calls again to see if he could find a new machine someone wanted to donate. He was careful to let Mr. Garcia know what was going on. This is the kind of thing Alphonso Lingis calls trust. "Trust is a break, a cut in the extending map of certainties and probabilities. The force that breaks with the cohesions of doubts and deliberations is an upsurge, a birth, a commencement. It has its own momentum, and builds on itself . . . like a river released from a lock, swelling one's mind and launching one on the way.

. . . To have put trust in . . . (someone) is to have to put still further trust in him. Once trust takes hold, it compounds itself."[15]

Living in the state of being "wide open," these guys can take on all the good and bad in the world at one time or another. But this is not a state of chaos or sheer negation. It's more like a work of initiating, calling out, instigating, inciting. Just to see what happens. Even if it's not much.

VITALITY

The surge that starts things. A cracking open, like a kernel that splits and becomes fecund. A crackling. A flashing up.

Durability. The property of being able to survive and grow.

AustinMama.com is an award-winning Internet zine for hardworking, sacrilegious mothers. Its art, poetry, and stories perform parenting as an affective charge that pulls people into places and forms that are far from predictable in the ideological standards of "good" and "bad" parenting.

AustinMama.com is funny and intimate. It sponsors gatherings like a Mother's Day spent sitting on lawn chairs in the parking lot of a hip store drinking cocktails and watching *Mommie Dearest*.

It drifts into identity practices—the naming and demonstrating of what it is to be "a mother." But then it breaks up "motherhood" into splintering affinities and differences (a common taste in books, a shared distance from mother-culture norms, a propensity for patience or rage). Then it drifts back into a looser, more affective, form of "mother" closure—an instance of hope, a feeling of connection to something big running through things. Or frantic depression or burnout.

The journal is eclectic. Its sensibilities range from wild adven-

[15] Alphonso Lingis, *Trust* (Minneapolis: University of Minnesota Press, 2004), 65.

tures in motherland (kids vomiting all over you all night, road trips thrown together on a whim) to inspirational words of wisdom gathered under the sign of "the mother," though not exactly without irony. Once, for instance, someone quoted Martha Graham on vitality: "There is a vitality, a life force, an energy, a quickening that is translated through you into action and because there is only one of you in all of time, this expression is unique . . . It is not your business to determine how good it is, nor how valuable it is, nor how it compares with other expressions. . . . You do not even have to believe in yourself or your work. You have to keep open and aware directly to the urges that motivate you. . . . There is no satisfaction whatever at any time. There is only a queer, divine dissatisfaction, a blessed unrest that keeps us marching and makes us more alive.[16]

FIREFIGHTERS

After 9/11 the figure of the firefighter became a vital one. The firefighters' bodies held a charge. They were inundated with gifts and letters. They went on "Thank You, America" bike tours, and women flocked to malls and parking lots just to get a look at them. They went through divorces, drugs, suicides. Some left their wives to marry other firefighters' widows. They suffered post-traumatic stress syndrome and World Trade Center syndrome. They complained about the stress of their mythic status. They said they were just doing their jobs. One man said he got the call to evacuate from the twenty-first floor, but he and other firefighters stayed in the lobby for another thirty minutes, helping people get out, until they heard the building coming down and jumped out thirty seconds before it fell. He said it was horrible, all the bodies falling.

[16] Agnes De Mille, *Dance to the Piper* (Boston: Little, Brown, 1952), 335.

He had no idea whether any of the others who had been in the lobby survived. He said that the only person he saved that day was himself and he did it by running like hell.

DEATH SIGHTINGS

Sometimes you can see death coming. There's a sad slackening of flesh and bone. The body shimmers as if shrouded. As if an energy that's moving through it is still vibrant but passing.

One day her father says he wants to talk to her. He's seventy-three and still working. It's the boom years of the stock market and he's been investing all of his income for retirement for the past few years. Suddenly there's money! It's as if he has some kind of secret genius to smell out what's happening. He's been watching the stock market channel. He's taken wild chances. (Her mother, on the other hand, remembers a spectacular failure or two. She worries that he'll go crazy and lose everything.)

Now there's money! She doesn't react much to this news. She's not sure what to say and she doesn't know that this is *the* moment for congratulations and good-byes.

Her father says he finally has all his papers in order. Something about a trust. He says he's been tired the last couple of days. Then the sad slackening comes. Suddenly his body is smaller, looser. It seems blurred, as if she's seeing him through water. She wants to shake her head and turn on more lights in the room as if there's something wrong with her eyes.

The next day he stays up late at the Christmas Eve party and then dies in his sleep on the living room pullout couch.

A blanket falls over everything. A massive ice storm kills half the trees on her father's beloved mountain. The men in the neighborhood murmur about how the trees snapping off in rapid fire all over the hills reminded them of enemy fire in Vietnam.

Later, she visits a friend who has just quit drinking again. He's perched on the edge of an old couch, hanging his head and shoulders down to his knees. He says he just can't start over again this time. Then the slackening comes. The edges of his body blur. He slumps way into the couch, as if half the water has suddenly been sucked out of his body.

They sit, suspended, for a long time. Then he closes his eyes and she turns to stare out the window.

The next day he's back. Miserable and scared. But the slackening has come and gone.

BORDER STORY 1

She remembers the oddly vital scene at the border one day when she was walking over the bridge into Nuevo Laredo. She expected the barbed wire fencing all along the bridge and the gruff treatment at the border crossing. But a scene of a young couple and their children washing their clothes in the river surprised her. The young man dove in. He swam down to the river bottom and then out across the wide expanse of water, halfway to the U.S. bank before he turned back. The water was sparkling in the sun. The breeze was blowing the clothes dry on the one scraggly bush on the bank.

Then she saw a group of about thirty men gather on the bank and draw together in a semi-circle around a speaker. The man in the center started to preach, cheering and clapping his hands. The others joined in. They all started to sing. She couldn't quite hear what they were singing but it was clearly inspirational.

Walking over the bridge to make the border crossing, the scenes below were like a mirage. But real too.

BORDER STORY 2

Marfa is a small west Texas town filled with (mostly white) ranchers, poor Mexican American farm workers, artists, and border patrol. She is sitting in a Mexican restaurant, listening to two older rancher couples talking about ranching troubles when three border patrolmen come in and sit down at the table next to her. There are border stories in national circulation about immigrants dying of thirst trying to cross the long, desolate stretch of desert that these guys patrol everyday. But these guys spend their lunch hour today swapping sweet, redemptive stories of rescuing wild animals on their patrol. Detailed, innocent stories. At first, she thinks this is some kind of crazy camouflage appliquéd onto the surface of the things these guys must do and see in the course of their day on border patrol. But then she realizes that the stories they're telling are about the animals they rescued that very day or earlier in the week, as if this is what they actually spend a lot of their day doing. She knows there are eccentric characters in Marfa whose lives revolve around sheltering rescued animals—there's the turtle man and the hawk woman and she is sure there are others—all with their trailers and yards and heads stuffed to overflowing with injured animals of that one kind. And listening to the border patrolmen tell their animal rescue stories adds an odd and simple excess to the heavily scripted image of the militarized border full of atrocities.

STILL WATCHING

On 9/11 she was living in Santa Fe. The talking heads were saying that everything had changed. But to her it seemed more like something had snapped into place that had been building for a long time. It's not like the shock in the ordinary was anything new. Here was the same rude awakening from an already fitful sleep. Then the double-barreled reactions of ponderous commentary and brash reaction. Then the dream of some kind of return to innocent slumber. Everyone was on alert. But there was also an undercurrent of deflation, like something buoyant had been beached.

She walked down to the neighborhood coffee shop to get the paper and rub shoulders with strangers in the intimate public of a national "we." The brilliant yellow daisies and blue asters hurt her eyes and the neighborhood still lifes blurred against the buzzing of her inner ear. The people at the coffee shop looked more tenderly fleshy. Their eyes were stunned, their cheeks puffy and pink.

She chained herself to the grid. But staying tuned in turned out to be an obsession shadowing her. She dreamed. She and her friend were fighting soldiers in a big field. Suddenly one of them cut off her friend's head. The dream action froze into a scene for emphasis. Pay attention! Her friend's body was standing in the field and her head was on the ground next to her as if it had grown up out of the ground like a pumpkin. The eyes in the head were moving back and forth, surprised and confused.

She took a day trip to Taos Pueblo's annual Saint's Day celebration. Fields of high grasses blew softly in the breeze. Dogs and horses were framed in quiet poses against blue mountains. The pueblo was full of grinning visitors. Native men wearing loincloths and body paint were running around snatching things from the native vendors' tables. They ran into the pueblo houses, kidnapped babies, and swung them, squealing, through the cold water of the river. With buckets of water they splashed spectators, who then lurched back into the crowd when they came near, frantically giggling and trying to avoid eye contact. It felt good not to have to know exactly what was happening. It was secret. Their business.

Inside the ceremonial circle, the religious leaders were waiting. It was beginning to storm. There was thunder and lightning, a cold rain and a fierce wind. Two strong men made the climb up a sixty-foot pole in the middle of the circle. At the top was a slaughtered sheep and two big, brilliantly colored sacks full of offerings. One of the men stood precariously on the top of the pole, untied an American flag from the back of his loincloth and held it in the wind over his head for a long moment, lightning flashing in the sky around him. It was amazing. Then he dropped the flag. One of the religious specialists snatched it out of the wind before it hit the ground. Who knew what it all "meant," but it was certainly an event in itself.

A fantasy crossed her mind of staying here; of being whatever this place was about. A mystery charged with potential.

DART GAME

A few weeks later, she went to the big annual dance at Jemez pueblo. At the entrance to the plaza, three weathered-looking white men were running an Osama bin Laden dart game. They were selling to teenage native girls the chance to shoot darts into bin Laden's face. Three darts for two dollars. They were shouting, "Everyone's a winner!" They were handing out American flags.

She watched. They watched her watching. Then she started to sidle up to ask them what this was all about. Their faces twisted like they were used to trouble. She slid back away from them without finishing her question and moved on, troubled in many directions at once.

The ordinary is a thing that has to be imagined and inhabited.

It's also a sensory connection. A jump.

And a world of affinities and impacts that take place in the moves of intensity across things that seem solid and dead.

She walks the neighborhood with Ariana in the very early morning, laying down imaginaries.

The yards are vulnerable in the predawn.

The mist rises in a yard full of playful and scary cement statues of giant bunny rabbits and gargoyles. What are these people doing with all these statues? They've built an ugly aluminum fence around them as if to protect them from theft. Or something.

Up the street, a large plastic ball is lodged in a tree.

The bird cries begin.

Ariana snatches flowers off bushes and drops them in her lap.

The vagueness or the unfinished quality of the ordinary is not so much a deficiency as a resource, like a fog of immanent forces still moving even though so much has already happened and there seems to be plenty that's set in stone.[17]

This is no utopia. Not a challenge to be achieved or an ideal to be realized, but a mode of attunement, a continuous responding to something not quite already given and yet somehow happening.

[17] The notion of the unfinished quality of the ordinary as a resource is from Rajchman, *The Deleuze Connections*.

This book is about how moving forces are immanent in scenes, subjects, and encounters, or in blocked opportunities or the banality of built environments.

It's also about the need for a speculative and concrete attunement. It suggests that thought is not the kind of thing that flows inevitably from a given "way of life," but rather something that takes off with the potential trajectories in which it finds itself in the middle.

It doesn't mean to come to a finish. It wants to spread out into too many possible scenes with too many real links between them. It leaves me—my experiment—with a sense of force and texture and the sure knowledge that every scene I can spy has tendrils stretching into things I can barely, or not quite, imagine. But I already knew that. The world is still tentative, charged, overwhelming, and alive. This is not a good thing or a bad thing. It is not my view that things are going well but that they *are* going. I've tried to let go of pat answers I never exactly believed anyway in an effort to stay in the middle of things.

Ordinary affect is a surging, a rubbing, a connection of some kind that has an impact.[18] It's transpersonal or prepersonal—not about one person's feelings becoming another's but about bodies literally affecting one another and generating intensities: human bodies, discursive bodies, bodies of thought, bodies of water.[19]

[18] Anna Tsing's *Friction: An Ethnography of Global Connection* (Princeton, N.J.: Princeton University Press, 2005) argues that the awkward, messy, unequal, unstable, surprising, and creative qualities of encounters and interconnection across difference should inform our models of cultural production.

[19] See Deleuze and Guattari, *A Thousand Plateaus*.

People are always saying to me, "I could write a book." What they mean is that they couldn't and they wouldn't want to. Wouldn't know where to start or how to stop. The phrase is a gesture toward a beginning dense with potential. They have stories, substories, tangles of association, accrued layers of impact and reaction. The passing, gestural claim of "I could write a book" points to the inchoate but very real sense of the sensibilities, socialities, and ways of attending to things that give events their significance. It gestures not toward the clarity of answers but toward the texture of knowing. What a life adds up to is still a problem and an open question; an object of curiosity.

Ariana is four now. She wants to do things for herself. She yells "*My* turn! *My* turn! Not-you-only-ME" when she's afraid that I won't give her the chance to try to read a book herself or to clean the cat's litterbox. Then she shifts into focus with a dry little cough. She has no idea whether she *can* do it, or even what it is, exactly, that she's trying to do. My mother, Claire, is recovering from a series of small strokes. She, too, sets off to do something for herself without knowing whether she can. Simple things take time, intensity, and ingenuity. Some things have to be sidestepped. Or solutions have to be invented. There are deadening frustrations but there's also a central, palpable pleasure in the state of trying. An impulse toward potentiality.

These impulses—Ariana's and Claire's—to "do it myself" are impulses toward the speculative. Like this book, they're only a beginning, just scratching the surface. But that's what matters in an ordinary saturated with affect's lines of promise and threat.

129

Barthes, Roland. *A Lover's Discourse*. New York: Hill and Wang, 1979.

———. *S/Z: An Essay*. New York: Hill and Wang, 1991.

———. "The Third Meaning: Research Notes on Some Eisenstein Stills." *The Responsibility of Forms: Critical Essays on Music, Art, and Representation*. Trans. Richard Howard. Berkeley: University of California Press, 1985.

Benjamin, Walter. *The Arcades Project*. Trans. H. Eiland and K. McLaughlin. Cambridge, Mass.: Harvard University Press, 1999.

Berlant, Lauren. "Cruel Optimism." *Differences* (forthcoming).

———. "Introduction." In *Intimacy*, ed. Lauren Berlant. Chicago: University of Chicago Press, 2000.

———. "Nearly Utopian, Nearly Normal: Post-Fordist Affect in *Rosetta* and *La Promesse*." *Public Culture* (forthcoming).

———. *The Queen of America Goes to Washington City: Essays on Sex and Citizenship*. Durham, N.C.: Duke University Press, 1997.

———. "Slow Death." *Critical Inquiry* (forthcoming).

Deleuze, Gilles, and Félix Guattari. *Anti-Oedipus: Capitalism and Schizophrenia*, vol. 1. Trans. Robert Hurley, Mark Seem, and Helen R. Lane. Minneapolis: University of Minnesota Press, 1983.

———. *A Thousand Plateaus: Capitalism and Schizophrenia*, vol. 2. Trans. Brian Massumi. Minneapolis: University of Minnesota Press, 1987.

De Mille, Agnes. *Dance to the Piper*. Boston: Little, Brown, 1952.

Hacking, Ian. *Rewriting the Soul: Multiple Personality and the Sciences of Memory*. Princeton, N.J.: Princeton University Press, 1998.

Harding, Susan, and Kathleen Stewart. "Anxieties of Influence: Conspiracy Theory and Therapeutic Culture in Millennial America." In *Transparency and Conspiracy: Ethnographies of Suspicion in the New World Order*, ed. Harry West and Todd Sanders. Durham, N.C.: Duke University Press, 2003.

Hosseini, Khaled. *The Kite Runner*. New York: Riverhead Books, 2003.

Jones, Edward P. *The Known World*. New York: HarperCollins, 2003.

Lingis, Alphonso. *Dangerous Emotions*. Berkeley: University of California Press, 2000.

———. *Foreign Bodies*. New York: Routledge, 1994.

———. "The Society of Dismembered Body Parts." In *Deleuze and the Theatre of Philosophy*, ed. Constantin Boundas and Dorothea Olkowski. New York: Routledge, 1993.

———. *Trust*. Minneapolis: University of Minnesota Press, 2004.

Lutz, Tom. *American Nervousness, 1903: An Anecdotal History*. Ithaca, N.Y.: Cornell University Press, 1993.

MacDonald, Andrew. *The Turner Diaries*. Fort Lee, N.J.: Barricade Books, 1996.

McEwen, Ian. *Atonement*. New York: Anchor Books, 2003.

Searcy, David. *Ordinary Horror*. New York: Viking, 2000.

Sedgwick, Eve Kosofsky. "Epidemics of the Will." In *Tendencies*. Durham, N.C.: Duke University Press, 1993.

Sparks, Nicholas. *The Notebook*. New York: Warner Books, 1996.

Stern, Leslie. *The Smoking Book*. Chicago: University of Chicago Press, 1999.

Stevens, Wallace. "July Mountain." In *Opus Posthumous: Poems, Plays, Prose*. New York: Knopf, 1989.

Stewart, Kathleen. "Arresting Images." In *Aesthetic Subjects: Pleasures, Ideologies, and Ethics*, ed. Pamela Matthews and David McWhirter. Minneapolis: University of Minnesota Press, 2003.

———. "Cultural Poesis: The Generativity of Emergent Things." In *Handbook of Qualitative Research*, 3rd ed., ed. Norman Denzin and Yvonna Lincoln. London: Sage, 2005.

———. "Death Sightings." *Cross Cultural Poetics* 3, no. 3 (2000): 7–11.

———. "Machine Dreams." In *Modernism, Inc.: Essays on American Modernity*, ed. Jani Scanduri and Michael Thurston. New York: New York University Press, 2002.

———. "The Perfectly Ordinary Life." In "Public Sentiments: Memory, Trauma, History, Action," ed. Ann Cvetkovich and Ann Pelegrini. Special issue of *Scholar and Feminist Online* 2, no. 1 (summer 2003).

———. "Real American Dreams (Can Be Nightmares)." In *Cultural Studies and Political Theory*, ed. Jodi Dean. Ithaca, N.Y.: Cornell University Press, 2000.

———."Still Life." In *Intimacy*, ed. Lauren Berlant. Chicago: University of Chicago Press, 2000.

———. "Where the Past Meets the Future and Time Stands Still." In *Histories of the Future*, ed. Susan Harding and Daniel Rosenberg. Durham, N.C.: Duke University Press, 2005.

Stewart, Kathleen, and Susan Harding. "American Apocalypsis." *Annual Review of Anthropology* 28 (1999): 285–310.

Taussig, Michael. *The Magic of the State*. New York: Routledge, 1997.

———. *My Cocaine Museum*. Chicago: University of Chicago Press, 2004.

This Is Nowhere. Missoula, Mont.: High Plains Films, 2000.

Thrift, Nigel. *Knowing Capitalism*. London: Sage, 2005.

Tsing, Anna. *Friction: An Ethnography of Global Connection*. Princeton, N.J.: Princeton University Press, 2005.

Waldie, D. J. *Holy Land: A Suburban Memoir*. New York: Norton, 1996.

Warner, Michael. *Publics and Counterpublics*. New York: Zone Books, 2003.

Williams, Raymond. *Marxism and Literature*. New York: Oxford University Press, 1977.

KATHLEEN STEWART
is an associate professor of anthropology and
director of the Americo Paredes Center for
Cultural Studies at the University of Texas, Austin.
She is the author of *A Space on the Side of the Road:*
Cultural Poetics in an "Other" America (1996).

Library of Congress
Cataloging-in-Publication Data

Stewart, Kathleen, 1953–
Ordinary affects / Kathleen Stewart.
p. cm.
Includes bibliographical references and index.
ISBN 978-0-8223-4088-1 (cloth : alk. paper)
ISBN 978-0-8223-4107-9 (pbk. : alk. paper)
1. Social psychology—United States. I. Title.
HM1027.U6S74 2007
302'.12—dc22   2007010609

CPSIA information can be obtained
at www.ICGtesting.com
Printed in the USA
FSHW021254161220
76947FS